Before Us On The Road
Passages From My Reading

William J. Dean

New York, New York

Before Us On The Road: Passages From My Reading
Copyright © 2019 by William J. Dean.

ISBN 9781098738181

Cover photo:
Beth Perkins/The New York Society Library, 2019,
Reading Stack 6, Fiction K-Z.

Dedication

This book is dedicated to writers "before us on the road" who have enriched our lives. The title comes from a letter written by Leigh Hunt, the English essayist, to the painter Joseph Severn, who was caring for Keats in Rome during his last days. "Tell him," Hunt writes, "he is only before us on the road, as he was in everything else...."

CONTENTS

INTRODUCTION..vii

PART ONE   Passages From My Reading.................1

PART TWO   Further Passages 39

PART THREE Among Favorite Writers..................85

            John Keats

            Albert Camus

            Gustave Flaubert

            Leo Tolstoy

            Joseph Brodsky

            Michel de Montaigne

            Samuel Johnson

            Charles Dickens

            Ignazio Silone

            Anton Chekhov

PART FOUR   Reading Passages (continued) 130

PART FIVE   Countrymen 140

            Benjamin Franklin

            George Washington

            Thomas Jefferson

            Abraham Lincoln

POSTSCRIPT 161

WRITERS
ENRICHING MY LIFE 163

ABOUT THE AUTHOR 167

ACKNOWLEDGMENTS 169

Introduction

At age 25, while a student at law school, I began the practice of writing favorite passages from my reading into a journal. I feared that by failing to do so, I would be unable to recall what had given me such pleasure.

I came to learn that others, long before me, going back to the Renaissance, and before, had done the same, and that collections of reading passages came, at some point, to be called commonplace books. A dictionary definition of the term: A personal journal in which quotable passages, literary excerpts, and comments are written.

When reading a book, I place light pencil marks in the margin next to passages of interest to me. Upon finishing, I go through the book again, copying these passages into my journal. What enormous pleasure I have in doing so, hoping to improve my writing skills by proximity to these wonderful writers, 125 by my count, who appear in this book and to whom this book is dedicated.

VIII   B<small>EFORE</small> U<small>S</small> O<small>N</small> T<small>HE</small> R<small>OAD</small>

My commonplace book is a treasure trove for me. Reading passages now fill 52 journal books. These occupy the top shelf of my bedroom closet. I read them over and over again. For a train trip, I take several journals with me to read selections as the train proceeds north along the majestic Hudson River. Or, when in Venice on the island of San Giorgio Maggiore, as cruise ships and tugs pass the Doge's Palace, there I am with journal in hand. And I do so on the East Green at 70th Street in Central Park across from the Frick Collection when seated on the grass leaning against the trunk of my favorite red oak. The passages deepen my life, and since I often read them aloud, enrich my use of the English language. In hundreds of my published essays I have drawn upon these passages.

In this book, at times I comment on why a passage is important to me. (My comments, as seems fitting, appear in smaller print than the luminous passages of the writers.) But in the spirit of W.H. Auden, in his commonplace book, A Certain World (1970), I do not comment on most of the passages. They speak for themselves. Auden writes, "I have tried to keep my reflections... to a minimum, and let others, more learned, intelligent, imaginative, and witty than I, speak for me."

But every passage I have selected for this book, and the many other passages I am not using to avoid an overlong book, is important to me. To invoke Auden once again, a commonplace book "is a sort of autobiography ....Here, then, is a map of my planet."

Most of the passages in the book appear the way they do in my journals, that is, in no order at all as to chronology or theme, shifting dramatically from tragedy to comedy, and back again — like life. I favor the anarchy of this approach, constantly surprising the reader. There are two exceptions, however. I have grouped passages on subjects of particular interest to me, such as war, teachers, music and Venice, and have matched some favorite writers, like Keats and Chekhov, to a cluster of passages from their own works.

In Sweet Theft, A Poet's Commonplace Book (2016), J. D. McClatchy refers to a Latin term for a commonplace book: silva rerum, "a forest of things." He eloquently concludes, "I hope you wander at will through my forest of things and take from it a part of the pleasure I had in transcribing what the leaves said and the birds sang."

Dear Reader, I hope my book will encourage you to do the same.

* * *

Postscript: A request for your indulgence. The passages in my commonplace book were selected by me over a period of 57 years in a variety of personal moods and different settings, using primitive writing instruments like defective pens and eraser less, unsharpened pencils. Through this lengthy process, I tried my best to be accurate when writing out passages. Also, for the extensive proofreading for this book, I had to work from my handwritten notes, not original texts.

To return to original texts for hundreds of selections would have added yet another decade to the project! Please remember, if you come upon errors, that my commonplace book was undertaken for pleasure and love of literature and the language, not as a doctoral dissertation.

PART ONE

Passages From My Reading

The First Man by Albert Camus.

Manuscript found in car following fatal crash.
Died January 4, 1960. 46 years old. Response of his
mother: "Too young." Book dedicated to her:
"To you who will never be able to read this book."
Mother deaf and illiterate. Father dies at age 29
in WWI. Camus very young. Years later, he reads
"on the tomb the date of his father's birth, which
he now discovered he had not known." My experience as
well. Much later I came to learn that father born in Godman,
Kentucky, May 29, 1891. Died in NYC, Dec. 3,
1936 of a heart attack, a month before I was
born. Mother a refugee from Russia at 16 and
widow at 33 with a two-year-old daughter and a
yet unborn son.

Camus: In The First Man "he

recaptures [his own] childhood and

not his father. He learns [as I came
to learn]
that he is the first man."

My reading notes on The First Man by Albert Camus.

Venice, January 1, 1500. Titian calling to Giorgione from a canal embankment:

Zorzo! Get up Zorzo! Our century has begun.

■ The youthful exuberance of two supreme painters at the start of the 16th century. Titian was to live 76 years into the new century; Giorgione, but ten. ■

It is suggested to Horace that he write no further verses. He responds:

I'll be hanged if that wouldn't be best. But I can't sleep all the time — No, it won't do. Everyone has his own way of enjoying himself. Mine is to put words into metre. No use talking about it. Whether peaceful old age awaits me or even now black-pinioned death flies round me, rich, poor, in Rome or, if chance bide, in exile, whatever my life shall be, bright or dark, I will write.

When I would bitterly complain about the dryness and boredom of learning the penal or mercantile codes by heart, he [the former dean of the University of Seville] would counter: "Forget the codes. Read Dostoevsky, read Balzac. That's all you have to know about criminal or commercial law." He also made me see that Stendhal was right that the best model for a well- structured novel is the Napoleonic Code of Civil Law.

                                        – Carlos Fuentes

■ At Columbia Law School, I felt as did Fuentes. My escape from "dryness and boredom" was undertaking a lengthy paper for a constitutional law professor on Thomas Jefferson and Chief Justice John Marshall. To do so, I shifted my venue from the law school at Kent Hall to Butler Library, bearing on its façade the names of great writers of ancient Greece and Rome. ■

> These faults of which you so complain
> Are part of human nature, I maintain,
> And it's no more a matter for disgust
> That men are knavish, selfish and unjust,
> Than that the vulture dines upon the dead,
> And wolves are furious, and apes ill-bred.
> — Moliére, The Misanthrope
> (translated by Richard Wilbur)

> The fog has been thickening
> into a bluish-grey blanket
> and blinding the sea she steals
> our clutch of archipelagos....
> She blurs away Chiloé,
> reaches down to Tierra del Fuego....
> — Gabriela Mistral

> May your magnificent heart rest, live, fight, sing and have off-spring in the Andean and ocean solitudes of our country.
> — Pablo Neruda on Mistral

■ Born in Chile in 1889, and christened Lucila de Maria Godoy Alcayaga, in her twenties she took the name Gabriela Mistral — the name of "an archangel and a fierce French wind" — writes Ursula K. LeGuin, who has translated her poems into English. For years, Mistral taught at schools in Chile. Neruda writes in his memoirs that she introduced him to the great Russian novelists. In 1945, Gabriela Mistral was awarded the Nobel Prize in Literature. Neruda received the prize in 1971.

I read Mistral's poems standing on the bridge of the "Magallanes" as the ship makes her way north along the Chilean coast from Tierra del Fuego to the island of Chilóe, past archipelagos, through fog-enveloped Pacific seas. Her poems seem to have been written for this voyage. ■

Night in Valparaíso! A speck on the planet lit up, ever so tiny in the empty universe. Fireflies flickered and a golden horseshoe started burning in the mountains. – Neruda

The life of the average human being on our planet is very difficult and very harsh. For me, this is the most important thing we are facing.... – Ryszard Kapuścińsk, Polish journalist and author

From the walls of Sangatte, a refugee center, now closed, used by migrants from the Middle East trying to cross the channel from France to England:

– My dear mother, forgive me for having abandoned you. I have taken all my desires with me
and have left you all my suffering.

– We have trapped ourselves. We are lost. We
have destroyed our home with our own hands;
we have become sorrow for our mothers, our
fathers, our neighbors.

Christ's commandment in Saint John:

Work while ye have the light.

Bookplate
Everyman, I will go with thee
and be thy guide,
In thy most need to go by thy side.

Madame de Staël noted that the word "enthusiasm"
has its roots from the Greek, meaning "god in us."

Human felicity is produced not so much by great
pieces of good fortune that seldom happen, as by
little advantages that occur every day.
                                    – Benjamin Franklin

Ubi caritas et amor,
Deus ibi est.

Where charity and love are,
There is God.

Still I can point to one or two things I have
definitely learned by being hard up. I shall
never again think that all tramps are drunken
scoundrels, nor expect a beggar to be grateful
when I give him a penny, nor be surprised if men
out of work lack energy.... That is a beginning.

— George Orwell,
Down and Out in Paris and London

■ Through my volunteer work as the Coalition for the
Homeless Wednesday night driver of the downtown
Manhattan food van, I came to learn much of what Orwell
had learned. I urged Mary Brosnahan, then executive
director of the Coalition, to read the Orwell book.

She did so and wrote: "Orwell's graphic firsthand account
of what it's like to be on the receiving end of charity... is
gripping and fascinating." Most memorable for her was
his description of a young man who appears regularly
and "without pretense or scolding" hands out food. She
generously wrote, his "forthrightness is noted by all in the
queue, as has Bill's for the last decade and a half.... So
thanks very much, Bill, to a man who quietly inspires the
rest of us to reach beyond our narrow limits and forge
community with those sleeping rough." Not so "quietly,"
dear Mary, since I was a bit of a chatterbox on the food
line, and, as my inclusion of your comment in this book
establishes, not above boasting. ■

A grasshopper landed on my shoulder smelled
like a pine. I had become a pine.

— Nikos Kazantzakis, Report to Greco

■ A grasshopper, a relation, perhaps, of the above, landed on my shoulder as I walked in Crete through a pine-scented forest to the sea, and then into the sea fully clothed, to recover from the intense heat. ■

> Blessed are those who are found studious of literature and Humane & polite accomplishments. Such have their lamps burning & such shall shine as the stars.   – William Blake

During World War II, Donald Keene was trained to translate Japanese documents. Among these documents were diaries found on dead Japanese soldiers. After the war, he turned to Japanese literature, ascribing his decision to "the close identification with the Japanese I had come to feel after reading their diaries and letters and talking with many prisoners." He studied and worked in Kyoto where "for the first time in my life, everything within me — my intelligence, my tastes, my emotions, my aspirations — all seemed to be pointing to the same direction."

> We have even survived a hundred years
>   of our own civil wars.
> These wars were prettily called
>   the Wars of the Roses —
> They were without decency or grace,
>   the opposing leaders were as alike as weeds.
> Men fought for no cause that is
>   intelligible to us now.
>   – Robert Lowell, Endecott and the Red Cross

I bring no doctrine, I refuse to give advice, and in an argument I immediately back down. But I know that today many are feeling their way tentatively, not knowing what to put their trust in. To them I say: Believe those who seek the truth, doubt those that find it, doubt everything, but don't doubt yourself.

– André Gide, La Séquestrée de Poitiers

It was a great mistake, my being born a man, I would have been much more successful as a sea gull or a fish. As it is, I will always be a stranger who never feels at home, who does not really want and is not really wanted, who can never belong, who must always be a little in love with death! (Edmund)

– Eugene O'Neill,
Long Day's Journey into Night

Closing lines from Ibsen's play, The Pillars of the Community:

Bernick: I have learnt that, too, these past days; it is women who are the pillars of the community.

Miss Hessel: Then you have learnt a poor kind of wisdom, my dear man. [Laying her hands firmly on his shoulders.] No, my dear; the spirit of truth and the spirit of freedom, they are the pillars of the community.

Recalling his nights spent writing, Robert Lowell in a letter to a friend:

How often it takes the ache away, takes time away.

Pound, Auden were dead: "The old boys drop like wasps from windowsill and pane." Lowell hoped to die as insects do in mid-autumn, "instantly as one would ask of a friend." He died in a taxi at age 60, on his way from Kennedy Airport to the city. This fragment was found among his papers:

Christ,
May I die at night
with a semblance of my senses
like the full moon that fails.

From Right You Are! (If You Think So) by Luigi Pirandello:

Closing line, Act I:
Laudisi (coming forward): So you want the truth, eh? The truth! The truth!
Hah! hah! hah! hah! hah! hah! hah! (Curtain)

Closing line, Act II:
Laudisi (coming forward): And there, ladies and gentlemen, you have the truth!
Hah! hah! hah! hah! hah! hah! hah! (Curtain)

Closing line, Act III:
Laudisi: Well, and there my friends, you have the
truth! But are you satisfied?
Hah! hah! hah! hah! hah! hah! hah! (Curtain)

■ Mother played the role of Laudisi when a student
at Radcliffe College in the early 1920s, learning this
important lesson for her future career in the field of
international relations: the elusiveness of truth. ■

ON MUSIC

But for the opera I could never have written
Leaves of Grass. My younger life was so
saturated with the emotions, raptures, up-lifts,
of such musical experiences that it would be
surprising indeed if all my future had not been
colored by them.

– Walt Whitman

We promise only to do our best and to live out
our lives. Dear God, that's all we can promise in
truth.... We're neither pure nor wise nor good.
We'll do the best we know.

– Richard Wilbur, the musical Candide

■ Mother concluded many of her lectures on international
relations with these lines. ■

I saw prisoners perform West Side Story at Sing Sing prison. How moving the words of Stephen Sondheim:

> There's a place for us,
> Somewhere a place for us.
> Peace and quiet and open air
> Wait for us
> Somewhere.
>
> There's a time for us,
> Some day a time for us,
> Time together with time to spare,
> Time to learn, time to care,
> Some day!
>
> Somewhere.
> We'll find a new way of living,
> We'll find a way of forgiving
> Somewhere.

From Verdi's opera, Don Carlo, based on Schiller's play:

> One day milder times will come and bring a better wisdom; then ordinary men will walk with kings and princes, the state will let its children dance, and human need once more will find a human heart to succor it. (Rodrigo, speaking to King Philip II of Spain, on behalf of the oppressed people of the Netherlands.)

Let me remind you that during the worst days of the blitz in London when the city was falling in rubble and ashes around the feet of its citizens, every day in the National Gallery — empty of course, because the pictures had been taken to safety — Myra Hess, the great harpsichordist, played Bach and Scarlatti and Mozart to anyone who cared to sit on the floor and listen. And the halls were crowded with quiet people in sanctuary, drawing salvation from what they heard. Oh proud! Oh gallant! They did this to show the world that they were not in the dust and to lift up their own hearts.

— Agnes de Mille,
dancer and choreographer

All the children must sing, and are divided by the teacher into canaries (the best singers), robins (fairly good singers), bluebirds (definitely not choral material), and pigeons (creatures who croak moodily upon one note).

— Robertson Davies,
The Table Talk of Samuel Marchbanks

■ My elementary school had been invited to sing at Carnegie Hall under the baton of Leopold Stokowski. At the final rehearsal, the music teacher came over and grimly looked me in the eye. "Dean, you're a croaker," denying me the opportunity to sing at Carnegie Hall under the Maestro's baton. ■

The Prussians march into Paris: "A magnificent morning with one of those bright suns that are indifferent to human catastrophes, whether they be called the victory at Austerlitz or the capture of Paris."
– Edmond and Jules de Goncourt,
Journal des Goncourt

■ Other tragic, magnificent sun-lite mornings: The fall of Troy. 9/11. ■

Whenever I leave a place now, a place where I've lived and worked, which has become a part of me — like Paris, Madrid, Toledo, El Paular, San José Purua — I stop for a moment to say adieu. "Adieu, San José," I say aloud. "I've had so many happy moments here, and without you my life would have been so different. Now I'm going away and I'll never see you again, but you'll go on without me.
– Luis Buñuel

Draft of a Memorial Plaque
A very long time later I came back to the grey immortal city. My feet timidly trod the spine of its stone-paved streets. They bore me up. You recognized me, you stones. Often, striding along wide lighted boulevards in foreign cities, I stumble in places where no one ever trips.

Passers-by turn in surprise, but I always know it's you. Rising suddenly out of the asphalt and then sinking back in, deep down....

Grandmother Selfixhe, Xhexho, Aunt Xhemo, Grandma, Kako Pino. All are gone. But at street corners, where walls join, I thought I could see some familiar lines, like human features, shadows of cheekbones and eyes. They are still there, frozen forever in stone, along with the traces left by earthquakes, winters, and human catastrophes.

– Albanian writer Ismail Kadare,
Chronicle of Stone

I have always lived (with involuntary interruptions) in the house where I was born, so my mode of living has not been the result of a choice. I believe that I represent an extreme case of the sedentary person, comparable to certain mollusks, for example limpets, which after a brief larval stage during which they swim about freely, attach themselves to a sea-rock, secrete an outer shell, and stay put for the rest of their lives.

– Primo Levi

■ I am a fellow mollusk, having lived on the same block and in the same apartment in New York City for 55 years ■

--------- TEACHERS ---------

Albert Camus, The First Man:

> In Monsieur Germain's class, they felt for the first
> time that they existed and that they were the
> objects of the highest regard: they were judged
> worthy to discover the world.... [H]e shared with
> them his philosophy but not his opinions... but
> he would condemn with all the more vigor those
> evils over which there could be no argument —
> theft, betrayal, rudeness, dirtiness.
>
> Upon receiving the Nobel Prize in 1957, Camus
> wrote Monsieur Germain: "When I heard the
> news, my first thought after my mother, was of
> you. Without you, without the affectionate hand
> you extended to the small poor child that I was,
> without your teaching, and your example, none
> of all of this would have happened."

Leonardo Sciascia, Sicilian Uncles. He writes of the
priest who provided his schooling:

> The little he taught me has been a good foundation
> for all that I've learnt and done, because not only
> did he teach me to read from an alphabet, to write
> a letter and not get confused over figures, he also
> taught me to find faith and companionship in
> nature, books and my own thoughts.

But above all, he said the Gospels were all he needed, and as he learned to know men from Guicciardini, so he had learned to love them from the Gospels. "And it's a difficult task," he said, "learning to love them, after having come to know them well."

Gaetano Salvemini to his geography teacher: "So we descend from worms?" The dear old man stopped and said quietly, "What harm would there be in that?"

■ Humphrey Fry taught English and history at St. Bernard's School, the elementary school I attended in New York City. He was tall and dignified, yet always approachable. He came to teaching late in life, having served in the British army and been a barrister. A highly educated man, he truly spoke and wrote the King's English. He could easily have taught at a university, but preferred teaching young children. How fortunate we were that he did. He cared for our well-being, revealing this in innumerable ways: in the detailed comments he made in his neat, precise hand in the margins of the scrawled chaos that constituted our attempts at prose; in the seriousness with which he approached teaching, as if it were a noble calling, and that we, for whom the effort was being made, must therefore not be without some significance; in his kind words of encouragement following an academic setback. Even in his critical remarks. They were never cutting, but expressed in the spirit of, "We both know you can do better than this." ■

At St. Thomas' College Boy School [in Sri Lanka] I had written 'lines' as punishment. A hundred and fifty times…, I must not throw coconuts off the roof of Copplestone House…. We must not urinate again on Father Barnabas' tires…. For years I thought literature was punishment, only a parade ground.

– Michael Ondaatje

■ Among the few poems I recite today, most were learned in detention. ■

It was the saints who baffled me. So I got to work on them as best I could…. Sebastian, that sanctified porcupine, was easy, and so was St. Roche, with the dog and a bad leg. I was innocently delighted to meet St. Martin, dividing his cloak, on a Swiss coin…. I was … a happy goat who had wandered into the wondrous enclosed garden of hagiology, and I grazed greedily and contentedly.

– Robertson Davies,
Fifth Business

Pope Francis calls upon priests to minister to their flocks: "to be shepherds with the smell of sheep…."

It's good to leave each day behind,
Like flowing water, free of sadness.
Yesterday is gone and its tale told.
Today new seeds are growing.
   – Jalaluddin Rumi, 13th century Persian poet

And the heart doesn't die when one thinks it
should.   – Czeslaw Milosz, Elegy for N.N.

Goethe on Mendelssohn's <u>Calm Sea and Prosperous
Voyage</u>: "Sail well in your music — may the voyage
always be as prosperous as this!"

I ... crossed the Alps on 9 May. Over the high
mountains the clouds hung like a great dark
curtain, and beneath these we drove through the
tunnel and, suddenly, found ourselves at Mira
Mara, where that marvelously bright light which
is the beauty of the south suddenly revealed
itself to me, gleaming like white marble. It was
to affect all my later work, even if the content
thereof was not always beautiful.
   – Michael Leverson Meyer, <u>Ibsen, A Biography</u>

Joan Miró, describing a visit, as a young man, to a
museum in Barcelona: 'There was a Monet landscape
in that show. It was so beautiful that when the guard
wasn't looking, I went over and kissed it.'

Cabbies were dozing by St. Mary's tower.
Kraków was tiny as a painted egg
Just taken from a pot of dye on Easter.
In their black capes poets strolled the streets.
Nobody remembers their names today,
And yet their hands were real once,
And their cufflinks gleamed above a table.
An Ober brings the paper on a stick
And coffee, then passes away like them
Without a name.

> – Czeslaw Milosz, Kraków in 1900

According to Plutarch... many of the Athenians
obtained their freedom, others who had already
escaped got food and shelter, by repeating
verses of Euripides, who was more popular
with the Sicilians than any other foreign poet.
The thanks of these survivors, many of whom
on their return [to Athens] expressed their
gratitude to him, were doubtless the sweetest
praise the poet ever had.

> – Thucydides

They [Emerson, Thoreau, Melville, Hawthorne,
Longfellow] have changed the shape of my
dreams....

> – Jorge Luis Borges,
> New England 1967

Nikolai Gogol visits typesetters during proof stage of
Evenings on a Farm Near Dikanka. Printer to Gogol:
"The items that you sent… have greatly amused the
typesetters".

Leo Stein, brother of Gertrude Stein, showed avant-
garde paintings of Matisse and Picasso, among others,
at Saturday Salons in Paris. He recalled proudly that
cynics "came to mock and remained to pray."

> I have provided no conversation for it [the Salad
> course]; one does not talk while eating Salad,
> one crunches.
> — Robertson Davies,
> The Table Talk of Samuel Marchbanks

> Men are "the brown-bread on whose crust I break
> my teeth, a bread of which I can never have
> enough…. Aye, those tousle-headed and good-
> for- nothings, how I love them."
> — Martin Buber

> May you have your wish and die in your sleep
> soon, Jim, darling. May you rest forever in
> forgiveness and peace. (Josie)
> — Eugene O'Neill,
> A Moon for the Misbegotten

Every soul should receive a toast from us for
bravery!

> – Hafez, Persian poet

The English camp at Agincourt. A common soldier:

But if the cause be not good, the King himself
hath a heavy reckoning to make, when all those
legs and arms and heads, chopped off in a battle,
shall join together at the latter day, and cry all,
"We died at such a place!"

> – William Shakespeare,
> King Henry the Fifth

King Henry IV of France: The temper of Henry's times?
In Paris, the St. Bartholomew's Day massacre of the
Huguenots. In the Netherlands, six thousand people
who would not abandon the Protestant faith being sent
to the block, gallows, or pyre. Elsewhere, Protestants
burning Roman Catholics. In the sixteenth century,
fanaticism was ecumenical. How gloriously out of tune
with his times were the words and deeds of Henry.

The words: "There must be no more distinction
between Catholics and Huguenots. All must be
good Frenchmen, and let the Catholics convert
the Huguenots by the example of a good life. I am
a shepherd king, who will not shed the blood of his
sheep, but seek to bring them together with kindness."

The deeds: When laying siege to Catholic Paris, he had not the heart to maintain too harsh a blockade, lest Paris become a cemetery. He celebrated the taking of the city with an amnesty, not executions. As soon as he was master of the city, one saw nothing but stonemasons at work. Henry was a builder king, two of his projects being the Pont Neuf and Place des Vosges in the Marais District. Henry IV is my favorite King of France.

> "I am the road running through Paris," says the Seine. "I have carried off many images since you were a child and reflected many clouds."
> – Julian Green, Paris

WAR

> If we took any period of a hundred years in the last five thousand, it has been calculated, we could expect, on average, ninety-four of those years to be occupied with large-scale conflicts in one or more parts of the world. This enduring, seemingly ineradicable fact of war is, in the Iliad's wise and sweeping panoramas, as intrinsic and tragic component of the human condition as our very mortality.
> – Caroline Alexander,
> The War That Killed Achilles

They sent forth men to battle,
But no such men return;
And home, to claim their welcome,
Come ashes in an urn.

For War's a banker, flesh his gold.
There by the furnace of Troy's field,
Where thrust meets thrust, he sits to hold
His scale, and watch the spear-point sway;
And back to waiting homes he sends
Slag from the ore, a little dust
To drain hot tears from hearts of friends;
Good measure, safely stored and sealed.

– Aeschylus, Agamemnon

Hecuba [What does war look like?]: Like the
bottom of a baboon. When the baboon is up a
tree, with its hind end facing us, there is the face
of war exactly: scarlet, scaly, glazed, framed in
clotted, filthy wig.

– Jean Giraudoux, Tiger at the Gates

"The Disasters of War" is a series of 82 etchings
created by Francisco Goya following the invasion
and occupation of Spain by Napoleon's army. Goya
selected a title for each etching. Both etchings and
titles convey the horrors of war:

– Is this what you were born for?
– There is no one to help them

– But they are of another breed
– Bury them and be silent
– One can't look
– Why?

I am Goya
of the bare field, by the enemy's beak gouged
till the craters of my eyes gape
I am grief

I am the tongue
of war, the embers of cities
on the snows of the year 1941
I am hunger

. . .

O grapes of wrath!
I have hurled westward
the ashes of the uninvited guest!
and hammered stars into the unforgetting
    sky — like nails
I am Goya

> – Andrei Voznesensky,
> translated by Stanley Kunitz

Almost a million Frenchmen had died since the Revolution, half of them under the age of 28. An English newspaper reported that shiploads of skeletons picked up on Napoleonic battlefields

had arrived in Hull to be crushed into fertilizer
— "the final by-product of Napoleon's victories.
fattening up English cows."
                              – Graham Robb, Victor Hugo

The fortunate reader, on occasion, comes upon a
book that "flings wide the gates of a new world." The
words are those of the French entomologist, Jean-
Henri Fabre (1823–1915), his reaction to an essay he
had just read on the habits of a wasp, and my reaction
when I came upon his writings. Fabre addresses the
subjects of his studies: "O my busy insects, enable me
to add yet a few seemly pages to your history." Each
insect is lovingly portrayed. The scarab beetle: "He
is smaller than a cherry-stone, but of an unutterable
blue. The angels in paradise must wear dresses of
that color." He describes himself as a self-appointed
inspector of spider webs. (Thoreau described himself
as self-appointed inspector of snow storms.)

■ Jean-Henri Fabre: Reverence for life in its many
manifestations. Napoleon: Grand Marshal of death. ■

From Virgil's The Aeneid, Book One (translation of
Robert Fitzgerald). Aeneas arrives at Carthage:

"What spot on earth,"
He said, "what region of the earth, Achatës,
Is not full of the story of our sorrow?
Look, here is Priam. Even so far away
Great valor has due honor; they weep here
For how the world goes, and our life
   that passes
Touches their hearts."

Dido welcomes the Trojans:

"Come, then, soldiers, be our guests. My life
Was one of hardship and forced wandering
Like your own, till in this land at length
Fortune would have me rest. Through pain
I've learned To comfort suffering men."

The hands of some tremble from age, sickness, or
drink.... They [the homeless of New York City]
must go out now into a world seemingly full of
people whose hearts are as hard and cold as the
pavements they must walk all day in quest of
their needs.... Then there is the worry of the
next meal or that night's sleeping arrangements.
Here starts their long weary trek to Calvary. They
meet no Veronica on their way to relieve their
tiredness, nor is there a Simon of Cyrene to
relieve the burden of the cross.
           – Dorothy Day, The Long Loneliness,
           co-founder of The Catholic Worker

Tennessee Williams' plays are about "the people who are not meant to win, the lost, the lonely, the strange, the difficult people who lack talons for the jungle."

Benjamin Franklin: Warned that America was "in no way what the French call a 'land of plenty' where the streets are paved with loaves of bread, the houses covered with omelettes and where already roasted chickens fly about crying, 'Eat me!'"

——— FIRST PUBLICATION ———

Dickens enters a bookshop on the Strand and asks for a copy of the Monthly Magazine. "Would his piece be there? .... Dickens turned aside to glance hastily and nervously through the pages. There it was! ... 'in all the glory of print.' So agitated that he wished only to be alone, he turned out of the crowded Strand and strode down the pavement of Whitehall to take refuge in Westminster Hall from the eyes of the pedestrians. There for half an hour he paced the stone floor '[his] eyes so dimmed with the pride and joy that they could not bear the street, and were not fit to be seen.'"

– Edgar Johnson,
Charles Dickens, His Tragedy and Triumph

Whitman, after submitting an early piece: "I remember with what half-suppressed excitement I used to watch for the big, fat, red-faced, slow- moving, very old English carrier, who distributed The Mirror in Brooklyn; and when I got one, opening and cutting the leaves with trembling fingers. How it made my heart double-beat to see my piece on the pretty white paper, in nice type."

– Gay Wilson Allen,
The Solitary Singer, A Critical Biography
of Walt Whitman

■ My waiting post at 11 p.m. was the newsstand at 79th Street and Second Avenue. Where, oh where, was The New York Times delivery truck with the issue carrying an article by me on the Op-Ed page? ■

The pay was measly, but for me there were the first pound notes I ever held in my hands, and I felt thrilled at putting into my pocket practically the same tender that was used by Dickens' and Joseph Conrad's characters.

– Joseph Brodsky

The Comte Greffulhe asks Marcel Proust to sign his guest book: "Just your signature, please. No comments."

From Mirror for Gotham: New York as Seen by Contemporaries from Dutch Days to the Present by Bayrd Still:

— John Adams (Fall 1774). We have been treated with assiduous respect; but I have not seen one real gentleman, one well bred man since I came to town. At their entertainments there is no conversation that is agreeable. There is no modesty — no attention to one another. They talk very loud, very fast, and altogether. If they ask you a question, before you can utter three words of your answer, they will break out upon you, again, and talk away.

— Walt Whitman: What can New York — noisy, roaring, rumbling, tumbling, bustling, stormy, turbulent New York — have to do with silence? Amid the universal clatter, the incessant din of business, the all-swallowing vortex of the great money whirlpool, who has any … idea … of silence?

The Autopsy

And so they found the gold of the olive-root
  had dripped in the recesses of his heart....

A little below the skin, the blue line of the
  horizon sharply painted....

His eyes open, proud, the whole forest moving
  still on the unblemished retina....

Only in the hollow of his left ear some light
  fine sand, as though in a shell, which means
  that often he had walked by the sea alone
  with the pain of love and the roar of the wind.

                                – Odysseus Elytis

Basis of tragic note found in Iliad and Greek
literature. This tension: Delight in life and clear
apprehension of its unalterable framework.
"As is the life of the leaves, so is that of men.
The wind scatters the leaves to the ground: the
vigorous forest puts forth others and they grow
in the spring-season. Soon one generation of men
comes and another ceases." Man is unique, yet for
all his qualities, he must obey the same laws as
the innumerable and indistinguishable leaves.

                                – H. D. F. Kitto,
                                The Greeks

Apollo to Poseidon: God of the earthquake,
you'd think me hardly sane if I fought with you
for the sake of wretched mortals... like leaves, no
sooner flourishing, full of the sun's fire, feeding
on earth's gifts, then they waste away and die.
                        – Homer, The Odyssey
                  (translated by Robert Fagles)

How strange that I should be called a destitute
woman! When I have all these treasures locked
in my heart. I think of myself as a very, very
rich woman! (Blanche)   – Tennessee Williams,
                          A Streetcar Named Desire

How would history judge a generation that, having
all the means to feed the earth's population,
refused to do so with fratricidal indifference?
What peace could be hoped for by people who
do not carry out the duty of solidarity?
                  – Pope John Paul II in Burkina Faso,
                                        West Africa

Again the shore, the woods,
The hills return to life.
The fountains and the sea
Hold converse with my heart.
            – Giacomo Leopardi, Il Risorgimento

I love my country with a singular love
That reason cannot move....

These things I love, and cannot tell you why.

Rivers in flood like seas,
Deep in her woods the swaying of the trees,
In the cold fields her silence — I love these.

And on the hill among the yellow corn
The two white birches shining in the sun....
              – Mikhail Lermontov, My Country

History says, Don't hope
On this side of the grave,
But then, once in a lifetime
The longed-for tidal wave
Of justice can rise up
And hope and history rhyme.
                   – Seamus Heaney, The Cure at Troy

I shall speak straight out because life is brief.
              – Andrei Sinyavsky (Abram Tertz),
                    A Voice from the Chorus

Why despair? For in the end, nothing hurts
my curiosity or my hope. I stop and wait with
endless patience at every twist and turn of life,

at every setback, at every cruelty; and if no sun
rises, I never believe it is night.

> – Michel Jobert,
> Memoires d'Avenir
> (Souvenirs of the Future)

The worst sinner has a future, even as the greatest
saint has had a past. No one is so good or so bad
as he imagines.

> – Sarvepalli Radhakrishnan,
> philosopher and
> president of India
> (1962-1967)

My brush,
Above me all the time, drips paint,
Turning my face into a perfect drop cloth.

> – Michelangelo

Blue mountains of Caucasus, I greet you!
You fostered me in childhood.

Eternity, o eternity! What is there
Beyond the celestial boundary of the world?
Tossed boundless ocean where the ages bear
No names or numbers; where lost stars are hurled
Aimless towards other stars....

> – Lermontov

—————————————— VENICE ——————————————

An angel appears:

| Pax tibi Marce | Peace be with you, |
| Evangelista Meus | Mark My Evangelist |

There is a glorious city in the Sea,
The Sea is in the broad, the narrow streets,
Ebbing and flowing; and the salt sea-weed
Clings to the marble of her palaces....
                                    – Samuel Rogers

For a Russian, poor and humiliated, it is not
hard to lose his mind here, in a world of beauty,
richness, and freedom.... There is a booming in
the air because of the pealing church bells. There
are streets as wide as the Nevsky Prospekt, and
there are some where, by spreading your arms, the
whole street can be blocked.... In short, he who
doesn't go to Venice is a fool....Crimea stacks up
against Venice as a cuttlefish against a whale.
                                    – Anton Chekhov

I remember one day — the day I had to leave
after a month here alone. I had just had lunch in
some small trattoria on the remotest part of the
Fondamente Nuove, grilled fish and half a bottle
of wine. With that inside, I set out for the place

I was staying, to collect my bags and catch a
vaporetto. I walked a quarter of a mile along the
Fondamente Nuove, a small moving dot in that
gigantic watercolor, and then turned right by the
hospital of Giovanni e Paolo. The day was warm,
sunny, the sky blue, all lovely. And with my back
to the Fondamente and San Michele, hugging the
wall of the hospital, almost rubbing it with my
left shoulder and squinting at the sun, I suddenly
felt: I am a cat. A cat that has just had a fish. Had
anyone addressed me at that moment, I would
have meowed. I was absolutely, animally happy.
                                  – Joseph Brodsky

And wherever I go, I carry the name of Venice
sculpted in my heart; I have always remembered
Venice; I have always sought to return. Every
comparison that I have the occasion to make
makes me see this place as more beautiful, more
magnificent, more respectable, and every time I
return I have discovered greater beauties, and
thus it will be also this time.
                          – Carlo Goldoni, One of the
                               Last Evenings of Carnival

It is a great oddity — a city for beavers – but to
my thought a most disagreeable residence.... I
soon had enough of it.
                          – Ralph Waldo Emerson

■ Mr. Emerson, we need to talk. I love Venice. "A city for beavers," indeed! The beavers in Concord, Mass., may be highly cultivated, but I doubt they appreciate the likes of Giovanni Bellini, Titian, Tintoretto, Veronese....

Were you aware that Venice began as desolate islands in a lagoon to which mainland refugees fled from the marauding Attila the Hun? And that over the centuries Venice became, "Lords and Masters of a Quarter and a Half-quarter of the Roman Empire," controlling the whole of the Eastern Mediterranean? Talk about self-reliance and improvement!

Magnificent art. Glorious architecture. Splendid light. These were here when you were here. In Venice, I awaken, as you would have, to the ringing of church bells and the arrival of ships from foreign ports, both East and West. At night, the lights of the city dance upon the dark canal waters. Sleep comes to me, as it did for you, with the sound of sea waves lapping the stone embankment. How could the magic of Venice elude you?

To your credit, you did come to Venice, unlike Mr. Thomas Jefferson. While serving as our minister to France, Jefferson traveled to Italy. He found time to smuggle rice seeds out of the country to benefit the American South — an act of agricultural espionage — but did not find the time to see the masterpieces of Palladio, the architect whose classical designs Jefferson called his "architectural bible".

Messrs. Emerson and Jefferson, I have great admiration for you both, but not on the subject of Venice. ■

NOTES

PART TWO

Further Passages

Turgenev's mother owned 5000 serfs.
Chekhov's father was born a serf and
did not acquire his freedom until his
~~teens.~~ teens. Chekhov writes of
himself, "[s]on of a serf...
who used his fists and tortured
animals...." What a transformation he
made in his life. Ernest Simmons writes,
~~even~~ even Tolstoy "never quite perceived
the breadth and tolerance of Chekhov's
Judgment, his tenderness for those who
suffered...." Chekhov squeezed
"the slave out of himself drop by
drop," something Solzhenitsyn
believed that every Russian living
under Stalinist rule needed to do.

Reading notes on Turgenev and Chekhov.

Oscar Wilde

The Ballad of Reading Gaol by C.3.3., Oscar Wilde's cell number at Reading Prison. His name did not appear on the book cover until the 5th edition. This work, he wrote, "is my chant de cygne, and I am sorry to leave with a cry of pain — a song of Marsyas, not a song of Apollo...."

> – Something was dead in each of us,
>   And what was dead was Hope.

> – I never saw sad men who looked
>   With such a wistful eye
>   Upon that little tent of blue
>   We prisoners called the sky,
>   And at every careless cloud that passed
>   In happy freedom by.

An Ideal Husband

> Lady Chiltern: Robert is as incapable of doing a foolish thing as he is of doing a wrong thing.

> Lord Goring: [After a long pause]. Nobody is incapable of doing a foolish thing. Nobody is incapable of doing a wrong thing.

> Lady Chiltern: Are you a Pessimist? What will the other dandies say? They will all have to go into mourning.

Lord Goring: [Rising]. No, Lady Chiltern, I am not a Pessimist. Indeed I am not sure that I quite know what Pessimism really means. All I do know is that life cannot be understood without much charity, cannot be lived without much charity. It is love, and not German philosophy, that is the true explanation of this world, whatever may be the explanation of the next....

Lady Chiltern: [Looking at him in surprise].

Lord Goring, you are talking quite seriously. I don't think I ever heard you talk seriously before.

Lord Goring: [Laughing]. You must excuse me, Lady Chiltern. It won't occur again, if I can help it.

Lady Chiltern: I like you to be serious.

Wilde is buried in the cemetery of Père Lachaise in Paris, beneath a monument bearing these words of his:

> And alien tears will fill for him
> Pity's long broken urn
>
> For his mourners will all be outcast men,
> And outcasts always mourn.

Remember all prisoners... and give them hope for the future.... Remember those who work in these institutions; keep them humane and compassionate; and save them from becoming brutal or callous.

– <u>Book of Common Prayer</u>

John Millington Synge in a curragh off the Aran
Islands in a bad sea:

> I thought almost enviously what fatiguing care
> I would escape if the canoe turned a few inches
> nearer to those waves and dropped me helpless
> into the blue bosom of the sea. No death were
> so delightful. What a difference to die here with
> the fresh sea saltiness in my hair than to struggle
> in soiled sheets and stifling blankets with a smell
> of my own illness in my nostrils and a half paid
> death tender at my side.

"The Splendour of Aton," composed to the sun god
Aton by the pharaoh, Akhenaten (ruled 1375-1358
BCE). Traveling by boat on the Nile at dawn, I read
aloud lines from the hymn:

> Thy dawning is beautiful in the horizon
>   of heaven,
> O living Aton, Beginning of life!
> When thou risest in the eastern horizon
>   of heaven,
> Thou fillest every land with thy beauty;
> For thou are beautiful, great, glittering,
>   high over the earth;
> Thy rays, they encompass the lands,
>   even all thou hast made...
> Though thou art afar, thy rays are
>   on the earth;
> Though thou art on high, thy footprints
>   are the day.

Jean Giraudoux

The Madwoman of Chaillot

- Countess: First the morning paper. Not, of course, these current sheets full of lies and vulgarity. I always read Le Gaulois, the issue of March 22, 1903 — it's by far the best... I'd gladly lend you my copy, but it's in tatters.

- Countess: You can let the mouse out of the trap. I'm tired of feeding it.

- Sewer Man: There's a lot of things come along that were obviously intended for us — little gifts, you might call them — sometimes a brand-new shaving brush — sometimes, The Brothers Karamazov....

- Countess: Do you know how to get in to speak to Madame Constantine? You ring twice, and then meow three times like a cat. Do you know how to meow?

- Countess: Before the deluge, you will recall, the Lord permitted Noah to speak in defense of his fellow mortals. He evidently stuttered.

Tiger at the Gates

- Ulysses: Understand me, Hector; you have my help. Don't ask me to interpret fate. All I have tried to do is read the world's hand, in the great lines of the desert caravans, the wake of ships, and the track of migrant birds and wandering peoples. Give me your hand. There are lines here, too. We won't search to see if their lesson tells the same story. We'll suppose that these three little lines at the base of Hector's hand contradicts the waves, the wings, and the furrows.

– Hector to the lawyer, Busiris: Discover a truth which saves us. What is the use of justice if it doesn't hammer out a shield for innocent people? Forge us a truth.

– Andromache: Everyone always dies for his country. If you have lived in it, well and wisely and actively, you die for it too.

Amphitryon 38

– Sosia, a slave: Sleep, Thebans! For it is good to sleep on the bosom of a land not ripped by the trenches of war, on unchallenged laws, among birds, dogs, cats, and rats who have not known the taste of human flesh. It is good to wear a national face, not as a mask to frighten those who have a different kind of skin or hair, but as the perfect oval for displays of smiles and laughter. It is good, instead of leaping up scaling-ladders, to climb towards sleep up a gentle stairway of lunches, dinners and suppers, to be free to wage in one's own heart, without qualms, the tender civil war of resentments, affections, and dreams. Sleep on!....

Jean Anouilh

The Lark

– Joan: Oh, Blessed Saint Michael, have pity on me. Have pity, Messire. Well, he didn't, and that was the day I was saddled with France. And my work on the farm.

– Joan: I say that true miracles are not tricks performed by gypsies in a village square. True miracles are created by men when they use their courage and intelligence that God gave them.

– Joan: He has done both good and evil, and thus twice acted like a man.

– Cauchon: And the time will come when our names will be known only for what we did to her; when men, forgiving their own sins, but angry with ours, will speak our names in a curse.

Antigone

Haemon: I love Antigone. She never struck a pose and waited for me to admire her. Mirrors meant nothing to her. She never looked at herself. She looked at me, and expected me to be somebody. And I was — when I was with her.

Eurydice

> Orpheus describing Eurydice's eyes: Just now,
> they're dark green, like deep water besides the
> stone steps of a harbor.

Ivan Turgenev

Chekhov's father was born a serf. Turgenev's mother
owned 5000 serfs, thousands of acres and 20 villages.

- I acquired my early loathing of slavery and
  serfdom by observing the shameful environment
  in which I lived.

- His mother: I cannot comprehend your desire
  to become a writer! Is that an activity for a
  gentleman? To my mind, a writer and a scribe
  are all the same…. Both scribble on paper for
  money…. A gentleman should serve the state
  and forge a career and a name for himself in
  that service, instead of blackening paper.

- Turgenev to Tolstoy: We have little in common. Your whole life is facing forward, mine
  is built on the past. It is impossible for me to
  follow you. And nor can you fall in with me.
  You're too far from me, and also you are too
  solidly planted on your own feet to become a
  disciple of anything….

– Attends a Molière play: The force, verve, freshness, the grace of the play literally flung me to the ground with my face in the dirt. After that, the quill drops from one's fingers.

– "Fortunate is he who on such a night has a roof over him, who has a warm corner of his own.... And Heaven help the homeless wayfarers...." (Chekhov quoting Turgenev in The Seagull.)

Joyce/Ibsen/Wilde

– Ibsen to William Archer, the translator of his works into English: I have read or rather spelt out, a review of Mr. James Joyce in the Fortnightly Review which is very benevolent and for which I should greatly like to thank the author if only I had sufficient knowledge of the language.

– Joyce to Archer: I wish to thank you for your kindness in writing to me. I am a young Irishman, eighteen years old, and the words of Ibsen I shall keep in my heart all my life. Faithfully yours, Jas A. Joyce. (To read Ibsen in the original, Joyce began to study Dano-Norwegian.)

– From Richard Ellman's biography, James Joyce: He [Joyce] took the occasion of his article to see in Wilde something of what he was coming

to regard as his own personality, the miserable
man who sings of joy.

Rainer Maria Rilke

- If your daily life seems poor, do not blame it;
blame yourself, tell yourself that you are not
poet enough to call forth its riches; for to
the creator there is no poverty and no poor
indifferent place.

- To a young poet seeking guidance: You cannot
disturb it [your development] more rudely
than by looking outward and expecting from
outside replies to questions that only your
inmost feeling in your most hushed hour can
perhaps answer.

- Think, Sir, of the world you carry inside you....

- Rilke on 1913 performance of play, Wozzeck,
by Georg Büchner (1813-37): A monstrous
affair. Nothing but the fate of a common
soldier... who stabs his faithless sweetheart, but
powerfully setting forth how, around the most
trivial existence, ... even around the recruit
Wozzeck all the greatness of existence stands....

- And now let us believe in the long year that is
given to us, new, untouched, full of things that
have never been.

Samuel Beckett

Waiting for Godot

– Vladimir: To all mankind they were addressed, those cries for help still ringing in our ears! But at this place, at this moment of time, all mankind is us, whether we like it or not. Let us make the most of it, before it is too late.

–Pozzo: He's stopped crying. You have replaced him as it were. The tears of the world are a constant quantity. For each one who begins to weep somewhere else another stops. The same is true of the laugh. Let us not then speak ill of our generation, it is not any unhappier than its predecessors. Let us not speak well of it either. Let us not speak of it at all.

– Estragon: I can't go on like this. Vladimir: That's what you think.

– Vladimir: Let us not waste our time in idle discourse! Let us do something, while we have the chance! It is not every day that we are needed!

– Beckett on his play, Krapp's Last Tape: Seventeen copies sold, of which eleven at trade prices to free circulating libraries beyond the sea. Getting known.

Giuseppe di Lampedusa

The Leopard

– The term 'countryside' implies soil transformed
  by labor, but the scrub clinging to the slopes
  was still the very same state of scented tangle
  in which it had been found by Phoenicians,
  Dorians, and Ionians when they disembarked
  in Sicily, that America of Antiquity.

– Do you really think, Chevalley, that you are the
  first who has hoped to canalize Sicily into the
  flow of universal history? I wonder how many
  Moslem imams, how many of King Roger's
  knights, how many Swabian scribes, how many
  Angevin barons, how many priests of the Most
  Catholic King have conceived the same fine
  folly; and how many Spanish viceroys too, how
  many of Charles III's reforming functionaries!

– [I]t was obvious at once that Vicenzino was
  'a man of honor', one of those violent cretins
  capable of any havoc.

– The two young people moved away, other
  couples passed, less handsome, just as moving,
  each submerged in their transitory blindness.
  Don Fabrizio felt his heart thaw; his disgust

gave way to compassion for all these ephemeral beings out to enjoy the tiny ray of light granted them between two shades, before the cradle, after the last spasms. How could one inveigh against those sure to die?

– [T]he stars were glittering away, producing thousands of degrees of heat which were not enough to warm one poor old man.

The Professor and the Mermaid

– The Mermaid: You are young and handsome; follow me now into the sea and you will avoid sorrow and old age … [A]nd remember that when you are tired, when you can drag on no longer, you have only to lean over the sea and call me; I will always be there, because I am everywhere, your thirst for sleep will be assuaged.

Bertolt Brecht

Life of Galileo

In the year sixteen hundred and nine
Science's light began to shine.
At Padua city, in a modest house
Galileo Galilei set out to prove
The sun is still, the earth on the move.

– Galileo: The moon is an earth with mountain and valleys — and the earth is a star. As the moon appears to us, we appear to the moon. From the moon, the earth looks something like a crescent, sometimes like a half-globe, sometimes a full-globe, and sometimes it is not visible at all.

– Old Cardinal: I am informed that Mr. Galilei transfers mankind from the center of the universe to somewhere on the outskirts. Mr. Galilei is therefore an enemy of mankind and must be dealt with as such. Is it conceivable that God would trust this most precious fruit of His labor to a minor frolicking star? Would He have sent His Son to such a place?

– Galileo: Why defend shaken teachings? You should be doing the shaking.... My work in the Great Arsenal of Venice brought me in daily contact with sailors, carpenters, and so on. These men are unread. They depend on the evidence of their senses. But they taught me many new ways of doing things. The question is whether these gentlemen here want to be found out as fools by men who might not have had the advantage of a classical education but who are not afraid to use their eyes. I tell you that our dockyards are stirring with the same high curiosity which was the true glory of ancient Greece.

– Can you see the Pope scribbling a note in his
diary: 'Tenth of January, 1610, Heaven abolished'?

– Andrea: [describing Galileo]: He put his
hands on his hams, stuck out his belly and said:
'Gentlemen, I beg reason!'

– Border guard: What's that book?
Andrea: It's by Aristotle, the great philosopher.
Border guard: (suspiciously). What's he up to?
Andrea: He's dead.

Florence Nightingale

She was conscious of the world of misery, suffering,
and despair which lay outside her little world of ease
and comfort.

– Florence Nightingale writes: "Dr. Howe, do you
think it would be unsuitable and unbecoming
for a young Englishwoman to devote herself to
works of charity in hospitals and elsewhere as
Catholic sisters do? Do you think it would be
a dreadful thing?"

– Dr. Howe responds: "My dear Miss Florence,
it would be unusual, and in England whatever is
unusual is thought to be unsuitable; but I say to
you 'go forward,' if you have a vocation for that
way of life, act up to your inspiration and you
will find there is never anything unbecoming or
unladylike in doing your duty for the good of

others. Choose, go on with it, wherever it may lead you and God be with you."

– Lord Napier visits her on board ship off Scutari in the Crimea: "I ... found you stretched on the sofa where I believe you never lay down again. I thought it would be a great happiness to serve you."

– Queen Victoria wishes to see Florence Nightingale's letters, "as I hear no details of the wounded...."

– A nurse describes Florence Nightingale on night rounds: "As we slowly passed along the silence was profound.... A dim light burned here and there. Miss N. carried her lantern which she would set down before she bent over any of the patients. I much admired her manner to the men — it was so tender and kind."

– She arranges to bring Alexis Soyer, Chef de Cuisine of the Reform Club in London, to improve the food for the troops in the Crimea. "He composed recipes for using the army rations to make excellent soups and stews... He invented ovens to bake bread and biscuits and a Scutari teapot which made and kept tea hot for fifty men. As he walked the wards with his tureens of soup the men cheered him. with three times three." (To this day, the Reform Club honors Soyer with the placement of his portrait in the dining room.)

– She receives an appeal from the Secretary of War in Washington to help the Union Army organize its hospital and care for the sick and wounded.

– She comments on plans for model cavalry barracks, suggesting that horses should be provided windows to look out of. An exasperated military doctor scribbles: "We have provided such a window and every horse can see out if he chooses to stand on his hind legs with his fore feet against the wall. It is the least exertion he can put himself to."

– Nurses would continue to write to Florence Nightingale after she returned from the Crimea, addressing her as Dear Mistress, Beloved Chief, Dearest Friend.

– At her burial, the coffin of Florence Nightingale was carried by six sergeants of the British Army.
– Cecil Woodham-Smith,
Florence Nightingale

Vincent Van Gogh

– What am I in the eyes of most people? A nonentity or an oddity or a disagreeable person — someone who has and will have no position in society, in short a little lower than the lowest.

– It's so painful for me to talk to most people, I'm not afraid to, but I know I make a disagreeable impression. Attempts to change that may well come up against the difficulty that the work would suffer if one lived differently.

– The Hague. A painter friend introduces Van Gogh to the public soup kitchens. He makes sketches.

– [T]hrough my work I'd like to show what there is in the heart of such an oddity, such a nobody.

– To the painter Mauve, who was mimicking him: "If you had spent night after night in the rain in London like me; if you had spent night after night in Borinage, hungry, homeless and feverish, you would have ugly lines on your face and a husky voice.

– I say, 'I can see that I shall become even more rough and unlovely, that I shall live in poverty, but I will be a painter.'

– I'd like to express something of life's struggle… in those gnarled black roots with their knots.

– [A] need continually to educate myself, to study, if you like, precisely as I need to eat my bread.

– Theo, his brother, thought that his passion for books meant that Vincent. had lost his feelings for pictures: "But you would be wrong in thinking I have lost my enthusiasm for Rembrandt or Millet or Delacroix or whoever it may be. On the contrary. You forget that we ought to love many things, and that they help each other to complete that love. There is something of Rembrandt in Shakespeare, of Correggio in Michelet, of Delacroix in Victor Hugo, and there is something of Rembrandt in the Bible, or the Bible in Rembrandt, whichever you please. So you must not think that I abandon my passions. Rather am I faithful in my unfaithfulness, and though I have changed outwardly I am inwardly the same, and my one desire as ever is to be of use in the world, to do good. This desire preoccupies me always. That is why I have been drawn to love and study pictures and now books."

– Departs from the leaden skies of Northern Europe for Provence: "What an opportunity! Nature here is so extraordinarily beautiful. It's the chance of a lifetime."

– I revel in … [the wheat fields] like a cicada.

▨ Van Gogh sees cypresses and oleanders, as did Petrarch. In Provence, I see wheat fields, olive groves and pines seen years earlier by Van Gogh, first seen by me in his works on museum walls. Late afternoon at the Monastery of St. Paul-de-Mausole. The olive grove is brimming with life. Butterflies, birds, cicadas, lizards. In the distance, the Alpilles. I lie in the field, reading aloud Vincent's letters to Theo. ▨

– At Saint-Maries-de-le-Mer: "At last I have seen
  the Mediterranean.... On the perfectly flat,
  sandy beach little green, red, blue boats, so
  pretty in shape and color that they made one
  think of flowers."

– Painting outdoors, Van Gogh contends with
  the strong Mistral wind: "I paint with the canvas
  flat on the ground while I kneel before it."

Anna Akhmatova

Her father asked her to use a pseudonym. She
chose the name of her Tartar great-grandmother
— Akhmatova, tracing her origin directly to Khan
Akhmat of the Golden Horde.

Tsarskoye Selo
A dark-skinned youth wandered
    along these allées,
By the shores of the lake he yearned,
And a hundred years later we cherish
The rustle of steps, faintly heard.

[The dark-skinned youth is Aleksandr Pushkin.]

Poems Without a Hero
Our separation is imaginary:
We are inseparable,
My shadow is on your walls,
My reflection in your canals....

Petersburg
But not for anything would we
    exchange this splendid
Granite city of fame and calamity,
The wide rivers and glistening ice,
The sunless, gloomy gardens,
And, barely audible, the Muse's voice.

I know that in this city [St. Petersburg] where
I have never lived, there had nevertheless been
deposited by some strange quirk of fate — a
previous life, perhaps? — a portion of my own
capacity to feel and to love, a portion — in other
words — of my own life; and that is something
no American will ever understand and no
Russian ever believe.

                        – George Kennan,
                        American diplomat

Vladimir Nabokov

– "Between the ages of ten and fifteen in St.
Petersburg," Nabokov writes, "I must have read
more fiction and poetry — English, Russian and
French — than in any other five-year period in
my life." Favorites included Chekhov, Tolstoy,
Keats and Flaubert. He read "War and Peace"
for the first time when he was eleven.

– One of his mother's "greatest pleasures in summer was the very Russian sport of <u>hodit po gribi</u> [looking for mushrooms]."

– He writes of his mother, "She found a deep appeal in the moral and political side of the gospels, but felt no need in the support of any dogma."

– He writes of the "mystery and enchantment" of "the illumination in the city [St. Petersburg] during imperial fêtes, when, in the padded stillness of a frosty night, giant monograms, crowns, and other armorial designs, made of colored electric bulbs — sapphire, emerald, ruby — glowed with a kind of charmed constraint above snow-lined cornices on housefronts along residential streets."

– Family lands and other valuables were confiscated during the Russian Revolution, but Nabokov inherited far greater wealth — what he called, "the beauty of intangible property, the unreal estate" of memories, language and literature. His "unreal estate" remained with him throughout his life.

From <u>A Letter that Never Reached Russia</u>:

– My happiness is a kind of challenge. As I wander along the streets and the squares and paths by the canal, absently sensing the lips of dampness through my worn soles, I carry proudly my ineffable happiness. The centuries will roll by, and schoolboys will yawn over the history of our upheavals; everything will pass, but my happiness, dear, my happiness will remain, in the moist reflection of a streetlamp, in the cautious bend of stone steps that descend into the canal's black waters, in the smiles of a dancing couple, in everything with which God so generously surrounds human loneliness.

■ Nabokov writes, "I was a perfectly normal trilingual child." So was my Russian-born mother who arrived in the United States in 1919 at age 16 as a refugee, her three languages being Russian, French and English, as were his. ■

Herman Melville

Bartleby, The Scrivener, A Story of Wall-Street:

The lawyer-narrator learns that Bartleby has no home and has been living in the law firm office:

> – Immediately then the thought came sweeping across me, What miserable friendlessness and loneliness are here revealed! His poverty is great; but his solitude, how horrible!

At times, the lawyer grows angry with Bartleby:

- But when this old Adam of resentment rose in me and tempted me concerning Bartleby, I grappled him and threw him. How? Why, simply by recalling the divine injunction: 'A new commandment give I unto you, that ye love one another.' Yes, this it was that saved me.

Having had Bartleby removed from his office, the lawyer visits Bartleby in the Tombs, the city's jail. The jailor and lawyer come upon his body:

- Jailor: Eh! — He's asleep, ain't he?
- Lawyer: With kings and counsellors, murmured I.

Melville concludes the story:
- Ah Bartleby! Ah humanity!

Billy Budd, Opera libretto by Benjamin Britten, E. M. Forster and Eric Crozier, adapted from Melville's story, Billy Budd, Sailor:

- Billy:

Billy Budd, king of the birds!
Billy Budd, king of the world!
Up among the sea-hawks, up against
the storms.
Looking down on the deck, looking
down on the waves.

Working aloft with my mates.
Working aloft in the foretop.

Billy strikes a malevolent officer who dies as a result.
Billy is sentenced to hang by Captain Vere.

– Billy:

Farewell to this grand rough world! Never more
shipmates, no more sea, no looking down from
the heights to the depths! But I've sighted a sail
in the storm, the far-shining sail that's not Fate,
and I'm contented. I've seen where she's bound
for. She has a land of her own where she'll anchor
for ever. Oh, I'm contented. Don't matter now
being hanged, or being forgotten and caught in
the weeds. Don't matter now. I'm strong, and I
know it, and I'll stay strong, and that's all, and
that's enough. Starry Vere, God bless you!

Captain Vere, years later, now an old man:

– We committed his body to the deep. The sea-fowl
enshadowed him with their wings, their harsh
cries were his requiem. But the ship passed on
under light airs towards the rose of dawn, and
soon it was full day — day in its clearness and
strength. For I could have saved him. He knew
it, even his shipmates knew it, though earthly
laws silenced them. O what have I done? But he
has saved me, and blessed me, and the love that
passes understanding has come to me. .... I was

lost on the infinite sea, but I've sighted a sail in the storms, the far-shining sail, and I'm content. I've seen where she's bound for. There's a land where she'll anchor for ever. I am an old man now, and my mind can go back in peace to that far-away summer of seventeen hundred and ninety-seven, long ago now, years ago, centuries ago, when I, Edward Fairfax Vere, commanded the *Indomitable*...

[The Curtain slowly falls]

Henry David Thoreau

– I had three chairs in my house; one for solitude, two for friendship, three for society. When visitors came in larger and unexpected numbers there was but the third chair for them all, but they generally economized the room by standing up.

– Enjoys gazing out of window overlooking kitchen garden, "particularly of a Sabbath afternoon, when all around was quiet and nature herself was taking her afternoon nap ...."

– I would rather sit on a pumpkin and have it all to myself than be crowded on a velvet cushion.

– Know your own bone; gnaw at it, bury it, unearth it, and gnaw it still.

– His neighbors' house was painted a unique yellow, "as if with pumpkin pies left over after Thanksgiving."

– In 1847 responds to an alumni questionnaire on 10th anniversary of his Harvard class: "I am a Schoolmaster — a private Tutor, a Surveyor — a Gardener, a Farmer — a Painter, I mean a House Painter, a Carpenter, a Mason, a Day-Laborer, a Pencil-Maker, a Glasspaper Maker, a Writer, and sometimes a Poetaster."

– Thoreau reverenced the title of traveler. "His profession is the best symbol of our life. Going from ____ to ____; it is the history of every one of us." When it came to less cosmic journeys, however, he rarely stirred from Concord and its environs. Indeed, he scorned foreign travels. "It is not worthwhile to go around the world to count the cats in Zanzibar."

From Thoreau's essay, "Walking":

– The sun sets on some retired meadow, where no house is visible, with all the glory and splendor that it lavishes on cities, and perchance as it has never set before — where there is but a solitary marsh hawk to have his wings gilded by it, or only a musquash looks out from his cabin, and there is some little black-veined brook in the midst of the marsh, just beginning to meander, winding slowly round a decaying stump. We walked in so pure and bright a light, gilding the withered grass and leaves, so softly and serenely bright, I thought I had never bathed in such a golden flood, without a ripple or a murmur to it. The west side of every wood and rising ground gleamed like the boundary of Elysium, and the sun on our backs seemed like a gentle herdsman driving us home at evening.

So we saunter toward the Holy Land, till one day the sun shall shine more brightly than ever he has done, shall perchance shine into our minds and hearts, and light up our whole lives with a great awakening light, as warm and serene and golden as on a bankside in autumn.

Ralph Waldo Emerson

Emerson's tribute to Thoreau:

– The scale on which his studies proceeded was so large as to require longevity, and we were the less prepared for his sudden disappearance. The country knows not yet, or in the least part, how great a son it has lost. It seems an injury that he should leave in the midst of his broken task which none else can finish, a kind of indignity to so noble a soul that he should depart out of Nature before yet he has been really shown to his peers for what he is. But he, at least, is content. His soul was made for the noblest society; he had in a short life exhausted the capabilities of this world; wherever there is knowledge, wherever there is virtue, wherever there is beauty, he will find a home.

– Look, look old mole! There, straight up before you, is the magnificent sun. If only for the instant, you see it.

– Emerson receives an unsolicited copy of <u>Leaves of Grass</u> from Whitman. He writes Whitman: "I find it the most extraordinary piece of wit & wisdom that America has yet contributed.... I greet you at the beginning of a great career...." [Emily Dickinson: You speak of Mr. Whitman — I never read his book — but was told he was disgraceful.]

Walt Whitman

Of <u>Leaves of Grass</u>, Whitman wrote:

– Remember, the book arose out of my life in Brooklyn and New York... absorbing a million people ... with an intimacy, an eagerness, an abandon, probably never equaled.

– Camerado, this is no book,
Whoso touches this touches a man.

– I sound my barbaric yawp over the roofs of
the world!

– Mannahatta! How fit a name for America's great
democratic island city! The word itself, how
beautiful! how aboriginal! How it seems to rise
with tall spires, glistening in sunshine, with such
New World atmosphere, vista and action!

City of ships!
(O the black ships! O the fierce ships!
O the beautiful, sharp bow'd steam-ships
and sail-ships!)

City of the world! (for all races are here;
All the lands of the earth make
contributions here;)

City of the sea! city of hurried and
glittering tides!

City whose gleeful tides continually rush or
recede, whirling in and out, with eddies
and foam!

City of wharves and stores — city of tall
façades of marble and iron!

Proud and passionate city — mettlesome,
mad, extravagant city!

> – Fifty years hence, others will see them
>   as they cross, the sun half an hour high,
>
> A hundred years hence, or ever so many
>   hundred years hence, others will see them,
>
> Will enjoy the sunset, the pouring in of the
>   flood-tide, the falling back to the sea
>   of the ebb-tide.

* * *

Thoreau on <u>Leaves of Grass</u>:

> – I have found the poem exhilarating, encourag-
> ing.... On the whole it sounds to me very brave &
> American.... We ought to rejoice greatly in him.

———————— INDEPENDENCE ————————

Thoreau: I would not have any one adopt my mode of living on any account; for, beside that before he has fairly learned it I may have found out another for myself. I desire that there may be as many different persons in the world as possible; but I would have each one be very careful to find out and pursue his own way....

Whitman: I had my choice when I commenc'd. I bid neither for soft eulogies, big money returns, nor the approbation of existing schools and conventions.... I have had my say entirely my own way....

Boris Pasternak

Doctor Zhivago

- I should like to be of use as a doctor or a farmer and at the same time to be gestating something lasting, something fundamental, to be writing some scientific paper or a literary work.

- The period confirmed the ancient proverb, "Man is a wolf to man."

- Life itself, the phenomenon of life, the gift of life is so breath-takingly serious.

- The main misfortune, the root of all the evil to come, was the loss of confidence in the value of one's own opinion. People imagined it was out of date to follow their own moral sense, that they must all sing in chorus, and live by other people's notions, notions that were being crammed down everybody's throat.

R. K. Narayan

My Days

- On a certain day in September, selected by my grandmother for its auspiciousness, I bought an exercise book and wrote the first line of a novel....

- Manuscripts returned: "The postman became a source of hope at a distance and of despair when he arrived."

- My first year's income from writing… about nine rupees and twelve annas.

- Piece accepted by Punch: This was my first prestige publication (the editor rejected everything I sent him subsequently) and it gave me a talking point with my future father-in-law.

Langston Hughes

The poems of Langston Hughes were popular with my students in Rajasthan, India, where I taught 7th, 8th and 9thgraders for four months in 2011. His poem, "The Negro Speaks of Rivers," resonates in a land of rivers. Hughes wrote the poem at age 19 in the summer following his graduation from high school.

> I've known rivers:
> I've known rivers ancient as the world and
>   older than the flow of human blood in
>   human veins.
> My soul has grown deep like the rivers.

Much of Rajasthan is desert. Few of my students had ever seen the sea. In his poem, "Long Trip," Hughes writes:

The sea is a wilderness of waves,
A desert of water....

Peak XV

1856 letter of Sir Andrew Scott Waugh, Surveyor-
General of India under British rule:

> We have for some years known that this
> mountain is higher than any hitherto measured
> in India and most probably it is the highest in the
> whole world.... The privilege as well as the duty
> devolves on me to assign to this lofty pinnacle
> of our globe a name whereby it may be known
> among geographers and become a household
> word among civilized nations.

> In virtue of this privilege, in testimony of my
> affectionate respect for a revered chief... and
> to perpetuate the memory of that illustrious
> master of accurate geographical research, I have
> determined to name this noble peak of the
> Himalayas Mont Everest.

Everest became a household word — the mountain,
not the man, George Everest. "But where history is
oblivious," writes the historian John Keay, "geography
is tenacious" by having placed his name, as it has done,
on every map in the world, and in the words of a later
superintendent of the survey, "just a little nearer the
stars than that of any other...."

Aleksandr Pushkin

Where are you, lovely Moscow of
    the hundred cupolas,
    Wonder of our land?
There where the solemn city reigned,
    Nothing but ruins remain....
    In gardens and in fields,
Where the scent of myrtle hung and
    lindens shook,
Now there are embers, ash and dust.
    Everything is dead, silence everywhere....
                    – Burning of Moscow, Age 15

Like the lamp that pales
In the dazzle of dawn,
False knowledge flutters and is consumed
By the sun of the mind.
Long live the sun! Down with night!
                        – Age 24

The pen calls for my hand, the page
    demands the pen;
Poetry then pours forth in
    lines of every hue.
Thus may a galleon stand,
    becalmed and sleeping, when
Suddenly comes the call!
    At which the scrambling crew

Swarms up and down to spread
   the swelling canvas wide.
The giant sallies forth, cleaving the
   Surging tide...
Where are we bound?

– Age 25

To be dependent on a monarch, or on
   the multitude...
To me, one is no better than the other.
   I want to live
My way, serve no one but myself and
   please no other,
Not bend my mind, my honor, or my knee
To any power or any livery. I want to go
Here and there, whenever my fancy leads,
To admire the divine beauty of this world,
Tremble with ecstasy, happiness, and love
For the creatures of art, for genius....

– A year before his death

No, I shall not die entirely! And my soul,
My lyre will outlive aches and the void....
I shall long be deemed congenial
For having taught my voice to sing
Of noble hearts, and freedom in a
   cruel age....

Mother introduced me as a child to Pushkin. At
home, she enjoyed reciting from Eugene Onegin to

an audience of two — my sister Elinor and me. She had memorized lines of his poetry when growing up in Saint Petersburg in pre-Revolutionary Russia.

Later, I learned about Pushkin's maternal great grandfather who, in the poet's words, was "stolen from the shores of Africa" by Turks and brought to Constantinople. At age 8, he was abducted by Russian agents and brought to the court of Peter the Great at a time when blackamoors were popular at European courts. Peter became his godfather and, in time, Abram Petrovich Hannibal became a major general, serving as chief of the Russian engineer corps. Pushkin's father came from one of the oldest families in Russia.

In 1837, Pushkin died in a duel at age 37. At the time Gogol wrote, "With him goes the greatest joy in my life." The 16-year-old Dostoevsky went into mourning. Pushkin was a favorite of Tolstoy and Chekhov. Turgenev said of Pushkin's contribution to Russian literature, "There is no doubt that he has created our language of poetry, our literary language...."

Only when I read the splendid book of Orlando Figes, Natasha's Dance, A Cultural History of Russia, did I understand the meaning of Turgenev's words, for prior to Pushkin, Russia barely had a national literature. In the last three-quarters of the 18th century, of 500 works of literature published in Russia, only seven were of Russian origin. Unlike England and France, Figes notes, in Russia there was a huge divide between the written and spoken languages. Pushkin filled the need to create a literary language rooted in the spoken language.

Pushkin expresses a preference for his grave site:

At the grave's portals, unrepining
May young life play, and where
I lie may heedless
Nature still be shining
With beauty that shall never die

Aleksandr Herzen

My Past and Thoughts, The Memoirs of Aleksandr
Herzen (1812-1870)

- Vera Artamonovna [his nanny] come tell me once
more how the French came to Moscow, I used to
say, rolling myself up in the quilt and stretching in
my crib, which was sewn round with canvas that
I might not fall out. Tales of the fire of Moscow,
of the battle of Borodino, of the Berezina, of the
taking of Paris were my cradle-songs, my nursery
stories, my Iliad and my Odyssey.

- We also had eight horses (very poor ones), but
our stable was something like an almshouse for
broken-down nags....

- "We are glad to do our best" was the formula
which Russian soldiers were expected to shout
when addressed on parade by a senior officer.

- The working people are still less hostile to
exiles: on the whole they are on the side of
those who are punished. The word 'convict'

disappears near the Siberian frontier and is
replaced by the word 'unfortunate'.

Orhan Pamuk

– My imagination… requires that I stay in the
same city, on the same street, in the same
house, gazing at the same view. Istanbul's fate
is my fate. I am attached to this city because it
has made me who I am.

– Ship horns, booming through the fog….

– I'd been counting the ships going up and down
the Bosporus. for some time. I'd been counting
the Romanian tankers, the Soviet warships,
the fishing boats coming in from Trabzon,
the Bulgarian passenger ships, the Turkish
Maritime passenger liners heading into the
Black Sea, … the elegant Italian ocean liners,
the coal boats, the frigates….

– When the ferry and the wind have changed
direction just slightly, the smoke rising from
the funnel begins to swoop and swirl over the
Bosporus like Arabic script.

– The storks flying south from the Balkans and
northern and western Europe as autumn nears,
gazing down over the entire city as they waft
over the Bosporus and the islands of the Sea of
Marmara ….

– The reddish-orange glint in the windows of Üsküdar at sunset....

– The mother of Orhan Pamuk had suggested he apply to medical school. "Instead, I tore Repin's portraits of Tolstoy and Dostoevsky out of a book and hung them on my wall."

William Maxwell

After 40 years, what I came to care about most was not style, but the breath of life.
– William Maxwell,
author and fiction editor,
The New Yorker

Stendhal

– On the first entry in his journal, makes a grammatical mistake. He is not concerned. "There will be a lot more, because I am making it a rule not to stand on ceremony and never to erase."

– If I were not afraid to be seasick I would gladly go to America.

– Occasionally when I bought a book I would write in it the date of purchase and a note on the feelings dominating me at the moment.

– If this book of mine is tedious, two years after
publication it will be used to wrap up parcels
of butter at the grocers....

– The man touched me, perhaps because I
realized that here was a human being more
unhappy than I.

– It seems to me that what prevented me from
ending it all was my curiosity in political
matters. Perhaps, too, without suspecting it, I
had some fear of hurting myself.

W. H. Auden

Plaque on St. Marks Place (East 8th Street) in New
York City:

> Wystan Hugh Auden
> Feb. 21, 1907 — Sept. 28, 1973
> Here lived, from 1953 to 1972,
> W. H. Auden, English poet and
>   American Citizen.
> "If equal affection cannot be,
> Let the more loving one be me."

– Time that is intolerant
Of the brave and innocent,
And indifferent in a week
To a beautiful physique,

Worships language and forgives
Everyone by whom it lives;
Pardons cowardice, conceit
Lays its honours at their feet.

– To say the least, every individual ought to know
at least one poet from cover to cover: if not as
a guide through the world, then as a yardstick
for the language.

Horace

– I am like the bee that busy works in the sweet
wild thyme around the groves and banks of
wide-watered Tiber. Even so small and toiling
hard like her I build my song.

– Asks of Apollo: Not rich grain lands in fertile
Sardinia, not gold nor ivory of India. Olives
are my fare and tender herbs from field and
garden. O son of Latona, give me to enjoy what
is mine — and with unweakened mind an old
age not uncomely or deprived of poetry.

– The swift moons can repair their losses in
the sky. We, when we are gone where the
great dead have passed, are dust and shadow.
Who knows if the gods will add tomorrow
to today.

Maxim Gorky

– Gorky: Doesn't God know everything?

His grandmother: If He knew everything, a lot of things that are done would not be done. It is as if He, the Father, looks and looks from Heaven at the earth, and sees how often we weep, how often we sob, and says: "My people, my dear people, how sorry I am for you!"

– Grandmother to Gorky: But it is not right to make fun of beggars. God bless them! Christ lived in poverty, and so did all the saints.

– I imagine myself, in my childhood, as a hive to which all manner of simple, undistinguished people brought, as the bees bring honey, their knowledge and thoughts about life, generously enriching my soul with what they had to give. The honey was often dirty and bitter, but it was all the same knowledge — and honey.

James Boswell

– London. At age 23, Boswell's dinner guests, Samuel Johnson and Oliver Goldsmith: I sat with much secret pride, thinking of my having such a company with me. I behaved with ease and propriety, and did not attempt at all to show away, but gently assisted conversation by those little arts which serve to make people throw out their sentiments with ease and freedom.... This evening I have had much pleasure. That is being truly rich.

– I can come home in an evening, put on my clothes, nightcap and slippers, and sit as contented as a cobbler writing my journal or letters to my friends. While I can thus entertain myself, I must be happy in solitude. Indeed there is a great difference between solitude in the country, where you cannot help it, and in London, where you can in a moment be in the hurry and splendor of life.

– [Johnson] advised me to keep a journal of my life, fair and undisguised.... I told him that I had done so ever since I left Scotland. He said he was very happy that I pursued so good a plan. And now, my journal! art thou not highly dignified? Shall thou not flourish tenfold? Johnson suggests burning after death. For my own part, I have at present such affection for this my journal that it shocks me to think of burning it.

– Boswell writes of Johnson that "He talked with uncommon animation of travelling into distant countries; that the mind was enlarged by it...."

– Boswell on his visits to Johnson: "From whence I had often a better and happier man than when I went in...."

Last words of Johnson to Boswell: "Fare you well!" Boswell writes in his Journal of the days following Johnson's death: "I recollect nothing."

– Boswell: How sad will it be, if I turn [out] no better than I am.

– James Boswell, Jr., age 16, to his father: "Pray, Sir, do not suffer yourself to be melancholy. Think not on your having missed preferment.... [T]hey who have obtained places and pensions have not the fame of having been the biographer of Johnson or the conscious exultation of a man of genius. They have not enjoyed your happy and convivial hours. They have not been known to Johnson, Voltaire, Rousseau, and Garrick. In short, would you, rather than have enjoyed so many advantages, have been a rich, though dull, plodding lawyer? You cannot expect to be both at the same time. Every situation in life has its advantages and disadvantages. Let me then have in your next letter a declaration that you are now in excellent spirits."

– Boswell responds to his son: "Before me lies your admirable letter of the 10th, in which you write de consolation like a true philosopher, who has observed human life and made just reflections."

Venice

- "Turner was seen in a boat near the island [of San Giorgio Maggiore] sketching the way the sunset lit up Palladio's great facade.... The backs of several of these studies are annotated with notes by Turner that testify to his excitement in being the temporary possessor of these views." my feelings precisely on each one of my 15 trips to Venice.

- There is a glorious City in the Sea, The Sea is in the broad, the narrow streets, Ebbing and flowing; and the salt sea-weed clings to the marble of her palaces.

  Samuel Rogers, Venice

- "And wherever I go, I carry the name of Venice sculpted in my heart; I have always remembered Venice; I have always sought to return."

  —Carlo goldoni, One of the Last Evenings of Carnival

Reading notes on my beloved Venice.

PART THREE

Among
Favorite Writers

John Keats

Keats arrives on the Isle of Wight:

> – I felt rather lonely this morning at breakfast so
> I went and unbox'd a Shakespeare — 'Here's
> my Comfort'.... [A]t this moment I am about
> to become settled, for I have unpacked my
> books, put them into a snug corner.

> – Pinned up Haydon — Mary Queen [of] Scots,
> and Milton with his daughters in a row. In the
> passage I found a head of Shakespeare which
> I had not before seen. It is most likely the
> same that George spoke so well of; for I like it
> extremely. Well — this head I have hung over
> my Books, just above the three in a row, having
> first discarded a French Ambassador — now
> this alone is a good morning's work.... [Upon
> his departure, Mrs. Cook, the landlady] made
> me take it with me though I went off in a hurry
> — Do you not think this is ominous of good?

■ God bless Mrs. Cook. By her generous act, she served
literature in a way few have done. ■

> – Tell George and Tom to write. — I'll tell you
> what — on the 23rd was Shakespeare born
> — now if I should receive a letter from you
> and another from my Brothers on that day
> 'twould be a parlous good thing — Whenever

you write say a Word or two on some Passage in Shakespeare that may have come rather new to you; which must be continually happening, notwithstanding that we read the same Play forty times…. I find that I cannot exist without poetry — without eternal poetry — half the day will not do — the whole of it — I began with a little, but habit has made me a Leviathan….

– [At Canterbury]. I hope the Remembrance of Chaucer will set me forward like a Billiard-Ball….

– It is unfortunate — Men should bear with each other — there lives not the Man who may not be cut up, aye hashed to pieces on his weakest side. The best of Men have but a portion of good in them….

– 24 April 1818. I was purposing to travel north this Summer — there is but one thing to prevent me — I know nothing I have read nothing and I mean to follow Solomon's directions of 'get Wisdom — get understanding' — I find cavalier days are gone by. I find that I can have no enjoyment in the World but continual drinking of Knowledge — I find there is no worthy pursuit but the idea of doing some good for the world — some do it with their society — some with their wit — some with their benevolence — some with a sort of power

conferring pleasure and good humour on all
they meet and in a thousand ways all equally
delightful to the command of Great Nature —
there is but one way for me — the road lies
though application study and thought.

– I carry all matters to an extreme — so that
when I have any little vexation it grows in five
Minutes into a theme for Sophocles.

– In Endymion, I leaped headlong into the Sea, and
thereby have become better acquainted with the
Soundings, the quicksand & the rocks, than if I
had stayed upon the green shore, and piped a silly
pipe, and took tea & comfortable advice.

– Notwithstanding the part which Liberals take
on the Cause of Napoleon I cannot but think
he has done more harm to the life of Liberty
than anyone else could have done; not that the
divine right Gentlemen have done or intend to
do any good — no they have taken a Lesson of
him, and will do all the further harm he would
have done without any of the good — The worst
thing he has done is, that he has taught them
how to organize their monstrous armies....

– [To his brother George in America]: I shall read
a passage of Shakespeare every Sunday at ten
oClock — you read one at the same time and
we shall be as near each other as blind bodies

can be in the same room.... Have you shot a
Buffalo? Have you met with any Pheasants?
My Thoughts are very frequently in a foreign
Country — I live more out of England than in
it — The Mountains of Tartary are a favourite
lounge, if I happen to miss the Allegany ridge,
or have no whim for Savoy.

– He expresses to George his great hope "that
one of your Children should be the first
American Poet" and writes of himself, "Though
I may choose to pass my days alone I shall be
no Solitary...."

– How astonishingly does the chance of leaving
the world impress a sense of its natural
beauties on us. Like poor Falstaff, though I do
not babble, I think of green fields. I muse with
the greatest affection on every flower I have
known from my infancy — their shapes and
colours are as new to me as if I had just created
them with a superhuman fancy — It is because
they are connected with the most thoughtless
and happiest moments of our Lives — I have
seen foreign flowers in hothouses of the most
beautiful nature, but I do not care a straw for
them. The simple flowers of our spring are
what I want to see again.

– To Fanny Brawne: "If I should die," said I to
myself, "I have left no immortal work behind
me — nothing to make my friends proud of

my memory — but I have lov'd the principle
of beauty in all things, and if I had had time I
would have made myself remember'd."

– Arrives in Naples: O what an account I could
give you of the Bay of Naples if I could once
more feel myself a citizen of this world....

Keats took lodging in Rome with the painter Joseph
Severn by the Spanish Steps. In 1959, at age 22, I
stayed at the Pensione Scalitena at the top of the
Spanish Steps. At the time I remember reading one of
Keats' marvelous letters in which he looked forward
to a walking tour in the north of England and Scotland
that will "make a sort of Prologue to the Life I intend
to pursue — that is to write, to study and to see all
Europe at the lowest expense. I will clamber through
the Clouds and exist." The letter pierced my heart.
Here we were, a similar age, both filled with hope
and vigor for the future, with a shared goal "to see all
Europe" and with the same practical consideration, "at
the lowest expense." But I knew, as he did not when he
wrote this letter, that his would be a short life.

– In his last letter to his close friend, Charles
Brown, he wrote from his sickbed by the
Spanish Steps: "I have an habitual feeling of my
real life having passed, and that I am leading
a posthumous existence. God knows how it
would have been — but it appears to me —
however, I will not speak of that subject.... I

can scarcely bid you good-bye, even in a letter.
I always made an awkward bow."

Following an eight-week period of confinement to
his room, Keats died on February 23, 1821, at the
age of twenty-five. From his room I go to the non-
Catholic Cemetery by Rome's ancient wall, near the
Pyramid of Gaius Cestius, where Keats is buried. In
the preface to "Adonais," his elegy on Keats, Shelley
describes the burial place as "an open space among
the ruins, covered in winter with violets and daisies."
Violets were his favorite flower. Keats' friends selected
these words for his gravestone: "Here lies One/Whose
Name was writ in Water." A robust epitaph would
have been more suitable. Perhaps these lines of his:

> But, when I am consuméd in the fire,
> Give me new Phoenix wings to fly
>   at my desire.

Teaching thirteen-year-olds in Rajasthan, India, I share
with them the story of John Keats who, at age 21, is
introduced by a friend to Homer through the English
translation of the "Odyssey" by the Elizabethan poet and
playwright, George Chapman. Returning late at night
to his London lodging, Keats writes of the experience:

> Then felt I like some watcher of the skies
> When a new planet swims into his ken;

Or like stout Cortez when with eagle eyes
He stared at the Pacific — and all his men
Looked at each other with a wild surmise —
Silent, upon a peak in Darien.

– On First Looking into
Chapman's Homer

"May you," I say to my students, "Come to share with Keats the experience of literary discovery."

Albert Camus

The Plague

- [H]e recalled that some thirty or so great plagues known to history had accounted for nearly a hundred million deaths.

- Nights and days filled always, everywhere, with the eternal cry of human pain.

- So I resolved always to speak — and to act — quite clearly, as this was the only way of setting myself on the right track.

- A loveless world is a dead world, and always there comes an hour when one is weary of prisons, of one's work, and of devotion to duty, and all one craves is for a loved face, the warmth and wonder of a loving heart.

– Grand: Oh, doctor, I know I look a quiet sort, just like everybody else. But it's always been a terrible effort only to be — just normal. And now – well, even that's too much for me.

– As a sort of postscript — and, in fact, it is here that Tarrou's diary ends — he noted that there is always a certain hour of the day and of the night when a man's courage is at its lowest ebb, and it was that hour only that he feared.

– And to state quite simply what we learn in a time of pestilence: that there are more things to admire in men than to despise.

– Tarrou: What's natural is the microbe. All the rest — health, integrity, purity (if you like) — is a product of the human will, of a vigilance that must never falter. The good man, the man who infects hardly anyone, is the man who has the fewest lapses of attention. And it needs tremendous will-power, a never ending tension of the mind, to avoid such lapses.

– Dr. Rieux asks Tarrou if he "had an idea of the path to follow for attaining peace." "Yes", he replied, "The path of sympathy."

– Nonetheless, he [Dr. Rieux] knew that the tale he had to tell could not be one of a final victory. It could be only the record of what had had to be done, and what assuredly would have to be done again in the never ending fight against terror and its relentless onslaughts, despite their personal afflictions, by all who, while unable to be saints but refusing to bow down to pestilences, strive their utmost to be healers.

The First Man

Dedicated to his mother, the Widow Camus: "To you who will never be able to read this book." The mother of Camus was illiterate. A childhood illness had left her deaf and speaking with difficulty. The family lived in Algiers in a working-class district. His father learned to read around age twenty. An uncle was partially mute, his grandmother illiterate. This was a family where few words were spoken. There was no oven. When they needed to bake, the dish would be taken to the baker, who, for a few centimes, would place the dish in the oven. There were no books at home.

> – ... and that if the poverty, the infirmities, the elemental need in which all his family lived did not excuse everything, in any case they made it impossible to pass judgment on those who were its victims.

> – Of the horses "that came from France; they were beaten down by the heat and the flies, and their eyes were those of exiles."

– On some evenings, it would sadden Jacques to look at them [fellow passengers on the trolley]. Until then he had only known the riches and the joys of poverty. But now heat and boredom and fatigue were showing him their curse, the curse of work so stupid you could weep and so interminably monotonous that it made the days too long and at the same time, life too short.

– And for all his life it would be kindness and love that made him cry, never pain or persecution, which on the contrary only reinforced his spirit and his resolution.

– Camus, with a friend, enters a public library: "Actually the contents of these books mattered little. What did matter was what they first felt when they went into the library, where they would not see the walls of black books, but multiplying horizons and expanses that, as soon as they crossed the doorstep, would take them away from the cramped life of the neighborhood."

– [H]e read on the tomb the date of his father's birth, which he now discovered he had not known.

– Life had all gone by without his having tried to imagine who this man was who had given him that life....

– From Camus' notes on this book: "Childhood continued — he recaptures childhood and not his father. He learns he is the first man."

Camus died in a car crash on January 4, 1960 at age 46. Comment of his mother when told of his death: "Too young." In the car was found the manuscript for The First Man. A few years earlier he had found the cemetery where he wished to be buried. "I'll be fine there," he wrote.

Gustave Flaubert

Madame Bovary

– What was it like, Paris? The very name had such a vastness about it! She repeated it to herself under her breath with a thrill of pleasure; it sounded in her ears like the great bell of a cathedral; it blazed before her eyes everywhere, glamorous even on the labels of her jars of pomade…. She bought a map of Paris, and with her fingertip she went for walks. She followed the boulevards, stopping at every corner, between the lines indicating the streets, in front of the white squares that were the houses. Then, closing her tired eyes, she would have a shadowy vision of gas lamps flickering in the wind and carriage steps clattering open in front of theatres.

– Language is like a cracked kettle on which we beat out tunes for bears to dance to, while all the time we long to move the stars to pity.

– Me and my books in the same apartment, like a gherkin in its vinegar.

– To Louise Colet: Twelve hours ago we were still together [in Paris] .... Now the night is soft and warm; I can hear the great tulip tree under my window rustling in the wind, and when I lift my eyes I see the reflection of the moon in the river.

– On the Nile: Somewhere, far away, on a river gentler and younger than this, I know a white house, and I know that its shutters are closed because I am not there. I know that the poplars, stripped of their leaves, are trembling in the cold mist, and that cakes of ice are drifting on the river and being thrown up against the frozen banks. I know that the cows are in their stable, that the espaliers are covered with their straw, and that from the farmhouse chimney white smoke is rising slowly into the grey sky.... In six weeks the trees will be budding, each branch will be studded with red. Then will come the primroses — yellow, green, rose, iris — decking the grass in the courts. O primroses, my pretty things, drop your seeds carefully, that I may see you another spring! I see the long wall hung

with roses, and the summerhouse beside the
water. A clump of honeysuckle grows outside,
climbing up over the wrought-iron balcony. At
one o'clock of a July morning, I like to fish there
in the moonlight.

– Yes, when I return I shall resume — and for a
good long time, I hope — my tranquil old life
at my round table, between my fireplace and
my garden. I shall continue to live like a bear,
caring nothing for my country, for critics, for
anyone at all.

– To Louise Colet: You and I are no longer
following the same route, we are no longer
sailing in the same skiff. May God lead each
of us where he wishes to go! I am not seeking
port, but the high seas. If I am shipwrecked,
you have my permission not to mourn.

--- FLAUBERT'S PARROT ---
by Julian Barnes

– From chapter, "The Case Against": [T]his
incredible weakness of character on my client's
part: he was on the whole against people killing
one another. Call it squeamishness, but he did
disapprove. He never killed anyone himself, I
have to admit, in fact, he never even tried. He
promises to do better in the future.

– Do you want art to be a healer? Send for the Ambulance George Sand. Do you want art to tell the truth? Send for the Ambulance Flaubert: though don't be surprised, when it arrives, if it runs over your leg....

– It's easy, after all, not to be a writer. Most people aren't writers, and very little harm comes to them. A phrenologist — that careers master of the nineteenth century — once examined Flaubert and told him he was cut out to be a tamer of wild beasts.

– So briefly: Flaubert teaches you to gaze upon the truth and not blink from its consequences; he teaches you with Montaigne, to sleep on the pillow of doubt; he teaches you to dissect out the constituent parts of reality, and to observe that Nature is always a mixture of genres; he teaches you the most exact use of language; he teaches you not to approach a book in search of moral or social pills — literature is not a pharmacopoeia; he teaches the pre-eminence of Truth, Beauty, Feeling and Style. And if you study his private life, he teaches courage, stoicism, friendship; the importance of intelligence, skepticism and wit; the folly of cheap patriotism; the virtue of being able to remain by yourself in your own room; the hatred of hypocrisy; distrust of the doctrinaire; the need for plain speaking. Is that the way you like writers to be described (I do not care for it much myself)? Is it enough? It's all I'm giving you for the moment: I seem to be embarrassing my client.

– May I die like a dog rather than hurry by a single second a sentence that isn't ripe!

– I breathe: it is a beautiful day, the sun sparkles on the river, at this moment a brig is passing in full sail; my window is open, and my fire is burning.

– George Sand upbraids Flaubert gently for being too harsh. Flaubert replies: "I work in the sincerity of my heart.... I do not heap up desolation for the fun of it. I simply cannot alter my eyes."

– I pass from exasperation to prostration, then I rise from annihilation to rage so that my mean emotional temperature is a state of annoyance.

– Let us sing to Apollo as in ancient days and breathe deeply of the fresh cold air of Parnassus; let us strum our guitars and clash our cymbals and whirl like dervishes in the eternal hubbub of Forms and ideas.

– I feel I'm liquefying like an old Camembert.

ГРАФЪ ЛЕВЪ НИКОЛАЕВИЧЪ
ТОЛСТОЙ.

My proudest possession: A print of Tolstoy inscribed to grandfather
who, in1909, visited Yasnaya Polyana, the Tolstoy estate, for several days
to record Tolstoy's voice for a gramophone company represented by
grandfather in Russia. (Note my unintended reflection in photograph.)

Leo Tolstoy

War and Peace

- Pierre was one of those people who, in spite of an appearance of what is called weak character, do not seek a confidant in their troubles. He digested his suffering alone.

- He [Prince André] felt happy and at the same time sad …. The chief reason was a sudden, vivid sense of the terrible contrast between something infinitely great and illimitable within him and that limited and material something that he …was.

- Prince Bolkonsky wishes to keep visitors away: "Has the snow been shoveled back"?

- Pierre's thoughts: But if you are alive — live: tomorrow you'll die as I might have died an hour ago. And is it worth tormenting oneself, when one has only a moment of life in comparison with eternity?

- Prince André, prior to the Battle of Borodino: And tomorrow I shall be killed… and the French will come and take me by my head and heels and fling me into a hole that I may not stink under their noses, and new conditions of life will arise, which will seem quite ordinary to others and about which I shall know nothing. I shall not exist.

– Pierre, a prisoner of the French: He glances up at the sky, and the twinkling stars in its faraway depths. "And all that is me, all that is within me, and it is all I!" thought Pierre. "And they caught all that and put it into a shed boarded up with planks!"

Anna Karenina

– Levin: He felt that he was himself, and did not want to be anyone else. All he wanted now was to be better than before.

– His [Levin's] unflagging craving to be better — she [Kitty] loved it in him....

– Levin to himself: No, ... you won't be any different, you'll be just as you've always been: full of doubts, perpetually dissatisfied with yourself, with futile attempts at self-improvement followed by lapses....

– The question of how to live had hardly begun to grow a little clearer to him when a new insoluble question presented itself — death.

– Levin felt the old impression of the club come back in a rush, an impression of repose, comfort, and propriety. He saw people of all sorts, old and young; some he knew a little, some intimate friends. There was not a single cross or worried-looking face. All seemed to have left their cares and anxieties in the porter's room with their hats, and were all deliberately getting ready to enjoy the material blessings of life.

– And Levin, a happy father and husband, in perfect health, was several times so near suicide that he hid the cord that he might not be tempted to hang himself, and was afraid to go out with his gun for fear of shooting himself. But Levin did not shoot himself, and did not hang himself; he went on living.

– I shall go on in the same way, losing my temper with Ivan the coachman, falling into angry discussions, expressing my opinions tactlessly; there will be still the same wall between the holy of holies of my soul and other people, even my wife; I shall still go on blaming her for my own terror, and being sorry for it; I shall still be as unable to understand with my reason why I pray, and I shall still go on praying; but my life now, my whole life apart from anything that can happen to me, every minute of it is no longer meaningless, as it was before, but it has an unquestionable meaning of goodness which I have the power to put into it.

* * *

– Tolstoy, in a letter to George Bernard Shaw: Indeed, my dear Shaw, life is a great and serious business, and each of us must contrive, in the brief time we have been allotted, to discover what our job is and do that job as earnestly as we can.

– Chekhov on Tolstoy's extraordinary efforts to organize several hundred food kitchens at a time of famine: Tolstoy — ah, that Tolstoy! In these days he is not a man but a superman, a Jupiter.

– From The Last Station by Jay Parini. On Tolstoy: He often weeps when music is played, either on the piano… or on the gramophone.

My proudest possession is a print of Tolstoy, inscribed by him to my grandfather. In 1909, grandfather spent several days with Tolstoy at Yasnaya Polyana, his country estate two hundred miles south of Moscow, to record his voice for a gramophone company represented by grandfather in Russia. Mother visited Yasnaya Polyana in 1964, as did I in 1973, a third generation visitor, a year following her death.

The house is modest. The dining room table is set. Grandfather described the food as very plain. Close by is a small table with a lamp. After dinner, guests and family would sit around the table as Tolstoy read passages from his most recent work. In Tolstoy's study I come upon his writing desk and the gramophone grandfather presented to him.

Tolstoy lies buried in a birch wood not far from the house. I walk to the grave in a gentle rain, called a "mushroom rain" by Russians. There is no monument, only an earth mound covered in leaves. When a child, Tolstoy had been told a story by his brother, Nicholas, that made a profound impression on him. Late in life, Tolstoy wrote, "I used to believe that there was a green stick on which words were carved that would destroy all the evil in the hearts of men and bring them everything good, and I still believe today that there is such a truth, that it will be revealed to men, and will fulfill its promise."

In his 82nd year, Tolstoy was buried where he believed the green stick lay.

Joseph Brodsky

– Once upon a time there was a little boy. He lived in the most unjust country in the world.... And there was a city. The most beautiful on the face of the earth. With an immense gray sky over that river. Along the river there stood magnificent palaces.... The wide river lay white and froze like a continent's tongue lapsed into silence.... And from the gray, reflecting river flowing down to the Baltic, with an occasional tugboat in the midst of it struggling against the current, I have learned more about infinity and stoicism than from mathematics and Zeno.

– Unlike both his predecessors and successors, this six-and-a-half-foot-tall monarch didn't suffer from the traditional malaise — an inferiority complex toward Europe.... In a way, geography was far more real for him than history, and his most beloved directions were north and west. In general, he was in love with space, and with the sea in particular. He wanted Russia to have a navy, and with his own hands this 'czar-carpenter' as he was called by contemporaries, built its first boat.... Tens of thousands found their anonymous end in the swamps of the Neva delta.... Carpenter and navigator, this ruler used only one instrument while designing his city: a ruler.

– In his youth, at least, a man born in this city spends much time on foot as any good Bedouin.... There is something in the granular texture of the granite pavement next to the constantly flowing, departing waters that instills in one's soles an almost sensual desire for walking. The seaweed- smelling headwind from the sea has cured many hearts oversaturated with lies, despair, and powerlessness. If that is what conspires to enslave, the slave may be excused. This is the city where it's somehow easier to endure loneliness than anywhere else; because the city itself is lonely.... When the crimson ball of the setting January sun paints their tall

Venetian windows with liquid gold, a freezing
man crossing the bridge on foot suddenly sees
what Peter had in mind when he erected these
walls: a giant mirror for a lonely planet.

– They [his parents] loved me more than
themselves.... The main issues were bread on
the table, clean clothes, and staying healthy.
Those were their synonyms for love....

– When I was twelve, my father suddenly
produced to my great delight a shortwave-
radio set. Phillips was the name, and it could
pick up stations from all over the world, from
Copenhagen to Surabaja. At least that was
what the names on its yellow dial suggested....
[The set had] a catlike, absolutely mesmerizing
green eye indicating the quality of reception....
To this brown, shining-like-an-old-shoe Phillips
set, I owe my first bits of English.... Through
the six symmetrical holes in the back, in the
subdued glow and flicker of the radio tubes, in
the maze of contacts, resistors, and cathodes, as
incomprehensible as the languages they were
generating, I thought I saw Europe. Inside, it
always looked like a city at night, with scattered
neon lights.

– The Tarzan series alone, I daresay, did more
for de-Stalinization than all of Khrushchev's
speeches at the Twentieth Party Congress

and after. One should take into account our latitudes, our buttoned-up, rigid, inhibited, winter-minded standards of public and private conduct, in order to appreciate the impact of a long-haired naked loner pursuing a blonde through the thick of a tropical forest with his chimpanzee version of Sancho Panza and lianas as means of transportation.

– [The winged lions of St. Mark in Venice.] Given my occupation, however, I've always regarded them as a more agile and literate form of Pegasus, who can surely fly, but whose ability to read is somewhat more doubtful. A paw, at any rate, is a better instrument for turning pages than a hoof.

– Judge: What is your profession?
Brodsky: Translator and poet.
Judge: Who has recognized you as a poet? Who has enrolled you in the ranks of poets?
Brodsky: No one. Who has enrolled me in the ranks of the human race?

– There is no other place in Russia where thoughts depart so willingly from reality: it is with the emergence of Saint Petersburg that Russian literature came into existence.... With two or three exceptions, all of them lived by the pen, i.e., meagerly enough to understand without exegesis or bewilderment the plight of those worse off as well as the splendor of those at the top.

– I am prepared to believe that it is more difficult for Russians to accept the severance of ties than for anyone else…. For us, an apartment is for life, the town is for life, the country in for life. The notions of permanence are therefore stronger; the sense of loss as well.

– In the context of the Russian life of those days, the emergence of St. Petersburg was similar to the discovery of the New World: it gave pensive men of the time a chance to look upon themselves and the nation as though from the outside.

– [The family apartment in Russia:] If space has a mind of its own and generates its own distribution, there is a chance some of these square meters, too, may remember me fondly. Now especially, under a different foot.

– [I]n the summer of 1977, in New York, after living in the country for five years, I purchased in a small typewriter shop on Sixth Avenue a portable 'Lettera 22' and set out to write (essays, translations, occasionally a poem) in English….

Michel de Montaigne

Reading preference of Captain Vere in <u>Billy Budd, Sailor</u>, by Herman Melville:

– "[H]is bias," Melville writes of Vere, "was toward those books to which every serious

mind of superior order occupying any active
post of authority in the world naturally inclines:
books treating of actual men and events no
matter of what era — history, biography, and
unconventional writers, like Montaigne, who,
free from cant and convention, honestly and
in the spirit of common sense, philosophize
upon realities."

– Montaigne becomes more revealing in his
Essays than he is face-to-face: "Amusing
notion: many things I would not want to tell
anyone, I tell the public; and for my most
secret knowledge and thoughts I send my
most faithful friends to a bookseller's shop."

– Others do not see you, they guess at you by
uncertain conjectures; they see not so much
your nature as your art. Therefore do not cling
to their judgment; cling to your own.

– Montaigne believed we should learn from what
we read, lest we be no better than "asses loaded
with books."

– To win through a breach, to conduct an embassy,
to govern a people, these are dazzling actions.
To scold, to laugh, to sell, to pay, to love, to
hate, and to deal pleasantly and justly with our
household and ourselves, not to let ourselves go,
not to be false to ourselves, that is a rarer matter,
more difficult and less noticeable.

– We are great fools. "He has spent his life in idleness," we say; "I have done nothing today." What, have you not lived? That is not only the fundamental but the most illustrious of your occupations, "If I had been placed in a position to manage great affairs, I would have shown what I could do." Have you been able to think out and manage your own life? You have done the greatest task of all. To show and exploit her resources Nature has no need of fortune; she shows herself equally on all levels and behind a curtain as well as without one. To compose our character is our duty, not to compose books, and to win, not battles and provinces, but order and tranquility in our conduct. Our great and glorious masterpiece is to live appropriately. All other things, ruling, hoarding, building, are only little appendages and props, at most.

– I have taken a road along which I shall continue… as long as there is ink and paper in the world.

– The concluding pages of the Essays are a hymn of gratitude for the joys of life. Some people consider life irksome and contemptible. Montaigne: "But I know it to be otherwise and find it both agreeable and worth prizing, even in its last decline, in which I now possess it; and nature has placed it in our hands adorned with such favorable conditions that we have only ourselves to blame if it weighs on us and if it escapes us unprofitably.... The shorter my possession of life, the deeper and fuller I must make it."

■ Montaigne in retirement resolved to record his thoughts so that he might "contemplate their ineptitude and strangeness." I place these words of his at the start of each column I write, lest anyone take me too seriously. ■

Samuel Johnson

– Johnson to Boswell: My dear friend, life is very short and very uncertain; let us spend it as well as we can.

– From preface to his Dictionary: "[L]et us make some struggles for our language."

– Sir, are you so grossly ignorant of human nature, as not to know that a man may be very sincere in good principles, without having good practice?

In the Dictionary entry under the verb, "to antedate," Johnson quotes essayist Jeremy Collier: "By reading, a man does, as it were, antedate his life, and makes himself contemporary with the ages past."

Writers of essays take note: Johnson defines essay as "a loose sally of the mind, an irregular indigested piece; not a regular and orderly composition."

– He who walks with vigor three hours each day will, in the course of seven years, cover a distance equivalent to the circumference of the earth.

– From the final issue of The Idler, an essay series written by Johnson: In every life there are pauses and interruptions… points of time where one course of action ends and another begins; and by vicissitude of fortune, or alteration of employment, by change of place or loss of friendship, we are forced to say of something, this is the last.

– We see a little, and form an opinion: we see more and change it. This inconsistency and unsteadiness, to which we must so often find ourselves liable, ought certainly to teach us moderation and forbearance towards those who cannot accommodate themselves to our sentiments.

– Good Friday, 1775. Johnson at 61: When I look back upon resoluti[ons] of improvement and amendments, which have year after year been broken… why do I yet try to resolve again? I try because Reformation is necessary and despair is criminal….

– Johnson on biography: If nothing but the bright side of characters should be shown, we should sit down in despondency, and think it utterly impossible to imitate them in any thing. The sacred writers related the vicious as well as the virtuous actions of men; which had this moral effect, that it kept mankind from despair.

– A man can write anywhere or anytime, "if he will set himself doggedly to it."

– Auden on Johnson: The utmost an artist can hope to do for his contemporary readers is, as Dr. Johnson said, to enable them a little better to enjoy life or a little better to endure it.

The stereotype of Johnson is that of a curmudgeon delivering crushing retorts. Aggressive by nature, he certainly relished victory in verbal confrontations. Overlooked are his many acts of kindness. His concern for the welfare of his copyists continued long after the publication of the Dictionary. To Shiels, often in financial distress, he sends money. He writes a preface to the elder Macbean's geography book to help promote its sale, and finds him a place in a home for "decayed gentlemen." He helps to arrange a theater benefit for Milton's indigent grand-daughter: "an opportunity… to secure the praise of paying a just regard to the illustrious dead, united with the pleasure of doing good for the living." He personally buys oysters for Hodge, his old and infirm cat, so that his servant "might not be hurt at seeing himself employed for the convenience of a quadruped."

Much of the time, Johnson is on the verge of financial ruin. A year after the publication of the Dictionary, he is writing to his friend, the novelist, Samuel Richardson: "Sir, I am obliged to entreat your assistance. I am now under arrest for five pounds eighteen shillings."

■ As my college graduation day approached, mother asked me to select a gift. I chose The Achievement of Samuel Johnson by Walter Jackson Bate, his course, "The Age of Johnson," being a favorite of mine at Harvard College. To this day, I regret not asking Professor Bate to inscribe the book. He would, I believe, have enjoyed doing so, and I know that his doing so would have given me immense pleasure. ■

Charles Dickens

David Copperfield

– From Dickens' preface to David Copperfield: Of all my books, I like this the best.... But, like many fond parents, I have in my heart of hearts a favorite child. And his name is David Copperfield.

– David: I was a posthumous child. My father's eyes had closed upon the light of this world six months, when mine opened on it.

– He [Mr. Peggotty] was but a poor man himself, said Peggotty, but as good as gold and as true as steel — those were her similies.

– Wherefore Mr. Micawber (who was a thoroughly good-natured man, and as active a creature about everything but his own affairs as ever existed, and never so happy as when he was busy about something that could never be any profit to him) set to work at the petition to the House of Commons praying for an alteration in the law of imprisonment for debt.

– "My dear," said Mr. Micawber, "Copperfield," for so he had been accustomed to call me of late, "has a heart to feel for the distresses of his fellow-creatures when they are behind a cloud...."

– David: Sleep came upon me as it came on many other outcasts, against whom house-doors were locked, and house-dogs barked, that night....

– "Never," said my aunt [Betsy Trotwood], "be mean in anything; never be false; never be cruel. Avoid those three vices, Trot, and I can always be hopeful of you."

– David thinks of the house where he grew up, now abandoned. I imagined how the winds of winter would howl round it, how the cold rain would beat upon the window-glass, how the moon would make ghosts on the walls of the empty rooms, watching their solitude all night.

– I may claim the merit of having originated the suggestion that the Will should be looked for in the box. After some search, it was found in the box, at the bottom of a horse's nose-bag; wherein (besides hay) there was discovered an old gold watch, with chain and seals, which Mr. Barkis had worn on his wedding-day, and which had never been seen before or since; a silver tobacco-stopper, in the form of a leg; an old horse-shoe, a bad shilling, a piece of camphor, and an oyster-shell.

– Betsy Trotwood to David: We must meet reverses boldly, and not suffer them to frighten us, my dear. We must learn to act the play out. We must live misfortune down, Trot!

– I confided all to my aunt when I got home; and in spite of all she could say to me, went to bed despairing. I got up despairing, and went out despairing.

– "My dear Copperfield," he [Micawber] replied. "To a man possessed of the higher imaginative powers, the objection to legal studies is the amount of detail which they involve. Even in our professional correspondence... the mind is not at liberty to soar to any exalted form of expression."

– The man who reviews his own life... had need to have been a good man indeed, if he would be spared the sharp consciousness of many talents neglected, many opportunities wasted, many erratic and perverted feelings constantly at war within his heart, and defeating him.

– I could not help but thinking, as we approached the [prison] gate, what an uproar would have been made in the country, if any deluded man had proposed to spend one-half the money it had cost, on the erection of an industrial school for the young, or a house of refuge for the deserving poor.

– ... and when boys came running after us, and got up behind [on the coach] and swung there for a little way, I wondered whether their fathers were alive, and whether they were happy at home.

– At these times, Mr. Micawber would be transported with grief and mortification, even to the length (as I was once made aware by the scream from his wife) of making motions at himself with a razor; but within half- an-hour afterwards, he would polish up his shoes with extraordinary pains, and go out, humming a tune with a greater air of gentility than ever. Mrs. Micawber was quite as elastic.

– Never shall I forget the lonely sensation of first lying down, without a roof above my head!

– I remember how the solemn feeling with which at length I turned my eyes away from looking at moonlight on the sea, yielded to the

sensation of gratitude and rest which the sight
of the white-curtained bed — and how much
more the lying softly down upon it, nestling in
the snow-white sheets! inspired. I remember
how I thought of all the solitary places under
the night sky where I had slept, and how I
prayed that I never might be houseless any
more, and never might forget the houseless.

■ Like David, I was a posthumous child. Five weeks before
my eyes opened, father's eyes closed forever, following
a heart attack at age 45. Mother became a widow at age
33. She raised my sister and me and never remarried.

I remember seeing an army trunk with father's name on
it. In the linen closet I came upon a bottle of bay rum he
used as shaving lotion. I learn the date and place of his
birth many years later: May 21, 1891, Godman, Kentucky.

Camus' father died in France during World War I when
Camus was a young child living in Algiers. Only decades
later, did he learn the date of his father's birth. In The
First Man, Camus concludes, with deep regret, that he
can never know his father, the first man in his life. I share
the same experience. ■

Ignazio Silone

Bread and Wine

– Every one of us is given the gift of life and
what a strange gift it is. If it is preserved
jealously and selfishly it impoverishes and

saddens, but if it is spent for others enriches and beautifies.

– No word and no gesture can be more persuasive than the life, and, if necessary, the death of a man who strives to be free, loyal, just, sincere, disinterested, a man who shows what men can be.

– He is saved who overcomes his individual egoism, family egoism, caste egoism, does not shut himself in a cloister or build himself an ivory tower, or make a cleavage between his way of acting and his way of thinking. He is saved who frees his own spirit from the idea of resignation to the existing disorder.... One must not be afraid, one must not be obsessed with the idea of security.

– The regulations for hotel-keepers were displayed behind the front door, but no provision had been made for the possible arrival of Jesus. "Tell me," said Matalena, "Supposing it really is Jesus, what ought we do? Tell the police?"

– So I went to Don Benedetto, not because he was a priest, but because in my eyes he has always been the pattern of the righteous man... He taught me that nothing is irreparable while life lasts, and that no condemnation is eternal.

– The hierarchy?
  God is at the head of everything.
  He commands in heaven.
  Everybody knows that.
  Then comes Prince Torlonia, ruler of the earth.
  Then come his guards.
  Then come his guards' dogs.
  Then nothing.
  Then more nothing.
  Then still more nothing.
  Then come the peasants.
  That's all.

* * *

– I don't know where to go...
  Neither do I...
  Then let's go together...

* * *

– As a boy he saw a handcuffed man limping
  down the road between two guards. "How
  funny he looks!" the boy cried. But his father
  took him by the ear and dragged him indoors,
  to be shut up in his own room. "What have I
  done wrong?" he asked, and received the reply:
  "You must never laugh at a convict."

  "Why not?"

"Because he can't defend himself. And then because, perhaps, he's innocent. And in any case, he's an unhappy man."

Anton Chekhov

The Cherry Orchard

– Lopakhin: The Lord God has given us vast forests, immense fields, wide horizons; surely we ought to be giants, living in such a country as this....

– Lubov Andryeevna: Oh my darling, my precious, my beautiful orchard! My life, my youth, my happiness... goodbye! .... Goodbye!

Uncle Vanya

– Astrov: I wondered whether the people who came after us in a hundred years' time, the people for whom we are now blazing a trail — would they remember us and speak kindly of us? No, Nanny, I'll wager they won't!

– Yeliena: It isn't a question of forests and medicine.... My dear, don't you understand? ... he's [Astrov] got talent! And do you know what that means? Courage, freedom of mind, breadth of outlook.... He plants a tree and wonders what will come of it in a thousand years' time, and speculates on the future happiness of mankind. Such people are rare, and we must love them.

Ivanov

– Sasha: ... let us run away to America.
Ivanov: I feel too lazy to walk to that door, and you talk of America!....

Lyebedev: You're talking nonsense, Count. Your business is to prepare to kick the bucket, brother — and mine, too.

Ivanov: No, Doctor, we all have too many wheels, and screws, and valves inside us to be judged by first impressions or by a few external traits. I don't understand you, you don't understand me, and we don't understand ourselves.

Three Sisters

–Vershinin: What shall I philosophize about now? .... [Laughs] Yes, life is difficult. It seems quite hopeless for a lot of us, just a kind of impasse....

– Masha: In time we shall pass on forever and be forgotten. Our faces will be forgotten and our voices, and no one will ever know how many of us there were.

Short Stories

- Life is only given us once, and one wants to live
  it boldly, with full consciousness and beauty.
                              – An Anonymous Story

- A prisoner dreams of owning a farm, marrying,
  having children. Naïve as his dreams were, they
  were uttered in such a genuine and heartfelt
  tone that it was difficult not to believe them….
  The constables listened and looked at him
  gravely, not without sympathy. They, too,
  believed in his dreams.   – Dreams

- [I]ncredible poverty all about us…. Yet all
  is calm and stillness in the houses and in the
  streets… [W]e do not see and we do not
  hear those who suffer, and what is terrible in
  life goes on somewhere behind the scenes….
  Everything is quiet and peaceful, and nothing
  protests but mute statistics: so many people
  gone out of their minds, so many gallons of
  vodka drunk, so many children dead from
  malnutrition… It's a case of general hypnotism.
                              – Gooseberries

- And he was charmed in the evening, the
  farmhouses and villas on the road, and the birch
  trees, and the quiet atmosphere all around,
  when the fields and woods and the sun seemed

preparing, like the workpeople now on the eve
of the holiday, to rest, and perhaps to pray ....
                                    – A Doctor's Visit

– He walked along thinking how frequently
  one met with good people, and what a pity it
  was that nothing was left of those memories.
  At times one catches a glimpse of cranes on
  the horizon, and a faint gust of wind brings
  their plaintive ecstatic cry, and a minute later,
  however greedily one scans the blue distance,
  one cannot see a speck nor catch a sound; and
  like that, people with their faces and their
  words flit through our lives and are drowned
  in the past, leaving nothing except faint traces
  in the memory.   – Verotchka

                    *   *   *

Chekhov writes of himself as being a "slave" in his
youth. "[S]on of a serf... who was whipped many
times... who used his fists and tormented animals...
who was hypocritical in his dealings with God and
men gratuitously, out of the mere consciousness of his
insignificance — write [he urges a colleague] how this
youth squeezes the slave out of himself drop by drop,
and how, waking up one fine morning, he feels that in
his veins flows no longer the blood of a slave but that of
a real man...." (Solzhenitsyn believed that every Russian
living under Stalinist rule needed, as Chekhov had done,
to squeeze "the slave out of himself drop by drop.")

– Anton Pavlovich graduated from the university
and a name plate reading DOCTOR A. P.
CHEKHOV appeared on our door.
        – Maria Chekhova, My Recollections

– To his younger brother Misha: Why do you refer
to yourself as an 'insignificant and inconspicuous
little brother?' So you consider yourself
insignificant? … Do you know before whom you
ought to be conscious of your insignificance?
Before God, perhaps the human intellect,
beauty, and nature, but not before men. Before
men you must be aware of your own worth.

– I'll write him [Aleksandr, his older brother] a
diplomatically — abusive — gentle letter.

– Chekhov on the night train, from Moscow to
Saint Petersburg, after Aleksandr wired that
he was severely ill. Chekhov writes to his
family from Saint Petersburg: "Generally, a vile
night…. My only consolation [on the train] was
my darling precious Anna (I mean Karenina)
who kept me busy all the way."

– A writer must "know that dunghills play
an important part in the landscape and evil
persons are as much part of life as good ones."

* * *

At age 30, Chekhov decides to visit the Russian penal
colony on Sakhalin Island, thousands of miles from

Moscow, off the coast of eastern Siberia. Letter
to Alexei Suvorin, his publisher: "You wrote that
Sakhalin is of no use or interest to anyone. Is that
really so? Sakhalin could be of no use or interest only
to a society that doesn't deport thousands of people
to it and doesn't spend millions on it.... Sakhalin is
a place of unbearable suffering, the sort of suffering
only man, whether free or subjected, is capable of."

Surnames assigned to prison exiles: Unremembered,
Countryless, Nameless, Man with Unknown Name,
Family Forgotten. Only one medical person in the
hospital on Sakhalin performs in a way not to "offend
the god Aesculapius by his attitude toward his duties."

Over a three-month period, Chekhov conducted
interviews with thousands of convicts. Of his book on
the experience, he wrote, "It gives me joy that this
harsh convict's robe shall have a place in my literary
wardrobe." He continued to correspond with convicts
over the years.

* * *

- Just as I'll be alone in my grave, so in essence
  shall I live alone.

- And now, shrinking from the cold, he thought
  that just such a wind had blown in the days of
  Rurik and in the time of Ivan the Terrible and
  Peter, and in their time there had been just the
  same desperate poverty and hunger, the same
  thatched roofs with holes in them, ignorance,

misery, the same desolation around, the same darkness, the same feeling of oppression — all these had existed, did exist, and would exist, and the lapse of a thousand years would make life no better.   – The Student

– But Chekhov reminds us that just as nature can change — "Look at this gorgeous, enchanted sky, at first the ocean scowls, but soon it, too, takes tender, joyous passionate colors for which it is hard to find a name in human speech" — so, too, can we change. "And however great was wickedness, ... everything on earth is only waiting to be made one with truth and justice, even as the moonlight is blended with the night."
                    – Gusev in the Ravine

– Help the poor. Take care of Mother. Live in peace among yourselves.
                    – From Chekhov's Will

■ Ah Chekhov, you who understand how difficult life is for most people. You who are generous in portraying those who strive to live a better life, even when they fail, which we mostly do. You who are modest, who never condemns. You who are tender towards those who suffer. ■

PART FOUR

Reading Passages
(continued)

Martha Graham to a dance student:

> – Hold your back straight, never forget that's
> where the wings grow.

Laca to Jenůfa in the closing moment of the opera:

> – Nothing matters if you are with me.
>   – Leoš Janáček, Jenůfa

Walking in New York leaves Walt Whitman "enrich'd
of soul, you give me forever faces".

Our Town

> Stage Manager: Babylon once had two million
> people in it, and all we know about 'em is the
> names of the kings and some copies of wheat
> contracts... and contracts for the sale of slaves.
>
> Stage Manager: Wherever you come near the
> human race, there's layers and layers of nonsense....
>
> Stage Manager: There are the stars — doing their
> old, old crisscross journeys in the sky. Scholars
> haven't settled the matter yet, but they seem to
> think there are no living beings up there. Just
> chalk... or fire. Only this one is straining away,
> straining away all the time to make something
> of itself. The strain's so bad that every sixteen
> hours everybody lies down and gets a rest.
>   – Thornton Wilder

[In the past few months] I have spent mortgaging my mares and colts one at a time to pay food and electricity and washing and such, and watching every mail train in hopes of a check. Now I have about run out of mules to mortgage.
                    – Selected Letters of William Faulkner

Giuseppe Verdi

Not every member of the public loved Aida. One dissatisfied customer wrote to the composer from Reggio, stating that he had travelled twice to Parma to hear the opera which, in his opinion, if it were not for the magnificent scenery, no audience would endure to the end. Claiming that the expense of these operatic excursions prayed on his mind like a terrible spectre, he enclosed an account for L. 31.80, the amount he had expended on two railway journeys, two opera seats, and two disgustingly bad dinners at the station. Verdi instructed his publisher to send the gentleman L. 27.80, having deducted the cost of the dinners which "he could perfectly well have eaten at home". He added: "Naturally he must send you a receipt, as well as a written undertaking not to attend another new opera of mine, so that he won't expose himself again to the dangers of being pursued by spectres or involve me in further travel expenses." The sum was paid, and the receipt and undertaking duly given.
                              – Charles Osborne,
                    The Complete Operas of Verdi

From Letters of Giuseppe Verdi, edited by Charles Osborne

- 23 November 1848. For six years I have been composing continually, wandering from country to country, and I have never said a word to a journalist or approached a friend or paid court to rich people in order to achieve success. Never, never! I have always despised means such as these. I write my operas as well as I can, and let things go their way without even trying to influence public opinions in the slightest.

- 5 June 1859. Put your hand on your heart and confess that I was a model of rare self-denial in not taking my score and going off in search of dogs whose barking would have been preferable to the sounds of the singers you offered me.

- 14 February 1883.
  Sad. Sad. Sad!
  Wagner is dead!

  When I read the news yesterday, I was, so to speak, horrified! Let us not discuss it! It is a great individual who has disappeared! A name that leaves the most powerful impact on the history of art.

Dostoevsky released from prison:

> – The fetters fell off I picked them up. I wanted
> to hold them in my hand, to look at them for
> the last time.....Freedom, new life, resurrection
> from the dead.....What a glorious moment!

Samuel Johnson on returning to Lichfield where he
had spent his youth:

> – I found the streets much narrower and shorter
> than I thought I had left them, inhabited by a
> new race of people, to whom I was very little
> known. My playfellows were grown old, and
> forced me to suspect, that I was no longer young.

Boswell:

> – To my question, whether we might fortify our
> minds for the approach of death, he [Johnson]
> answered in a passion, "No, sir, let it alone. It
> matters not how a man dies, but how he lives."

* * *

They told me, Heraclitus, they told me you
    were dead,
They brought me bitter news to hear and
    bitter tears to shed.
I wept as I remember' d, how often you and I
Had tired the sun with talking and sent him
    down the sky.

And now that thou art lying, my dear old
    Carian guest,
A handful of grey ashes, long, long ago at rest,
Still are thy pleasant voices, thy nightingales,
    awake;
For Death, he taketh all away, but them he
    cannot take.
                    – William Johnson Cory, Heraclitus

Keats while a student at medical school:

– The other day... during a lecture, there came
  a sunbeam into the room, and with it a whole
  troop of creatures floating in the ray; and I was
  off with them to Oberon and fairyland.

Honoré Balzac

– Balzac to his sister, Laure: Do you know,
  I've spent a whole week ruminating and
  broodulating and eatulating and strollulating
  without doing anything useful.

– Balzac to Laure: Fire broke out in this quarter
  at 9 Rue des Lesdiquieres, in the head of a
  young man on the fifth floor. The fire brigade
  have been working on it for a month and a
  half, but there's no putting it out. The young
  man is consumed with a passion for a beautiful
  woman he has not met. She is called Fame....

Martin Buber

– You shall not withhold yourself.

You, imprisoned in the shells in which society, state, church, school, economy, public opinion, and your own pride have stuck you, indirect one among indirect ones, break through your shells, become direct; man, have contact with men!

– A teacher meets a face which strikes him: "It is not a beautiful face nor particularly intelligent; but it is a real face, or, rather, the chaos preceding the cosmos of a real face."

Winston Churchill

By being so long in the lowest form [at Harrow], I gained an immense advantage over the cleverer boys. They all went on to learn Latin and Greek and splendid things like that. But I was taught English. I got into my bones the essential structure of an ordinary English sentence — which is a noble thing.

Franklin D. Roosevelt

An artillery range in the Yellowstone Park Area threatened the existence of the last of North America's largest waterfowl — the Trumpeter Swan. President to the Secretary of War:

– The verdict is for the Trumpeter Swan and against the Army. The Army must find a different nesting place.

– Adolph Brandeis arrived from Prague in the fall of 1848 to explore moving his family to the United States. Months after arriving, he wrote to his wife:

> – I already love our country so much, that I rejoice when I can sing its praises......I have gotten hold of a book which contains the messages of all the Presidents. This week I have been reading of the progress made in Washington's day, and I felt as proud and happy about it as though it had been my own doing.

Husband and wife chose to move here. Many years later, their son, Louis, became a justice of the United States Supreme Court.

– Elizabeth, the Queen Mother, during the bombing of London:

> – The Princesses could not leave without me — and I could never leave without the King — and, of course, the King will never leave.

– Mahatma Gandhi:

> – I do not want my house to be walled in on all sides and my windows stuffed. I want the cultures of all lands to be blown about my house as freely as possible. But I refuse to be blown off my feet by any.

Thoreau

– I went to the woods because I wished to live deliberately, to front only the essential facts of life, and see if I could not learn what it had to teach, and not, when I came to die, discover that I had not lived. I did not wish to live what was not life, living is so dear I wanted to live deep and seek out all the marrow of life.

– I learned this at least by my experiment: that if one advances confidently in the direction of his dreams, and endeavors to live the life which he has imagined, he will meet with a success unexpected in common hours.

– The youth gets together his materials to build a bridge to the moon, or perchance, a palace or temple on the earth, and, at length, the middle-aged man concludes to build a woodshed with them.

– Prime Minister Melbourne to his departing colleagues after a lengthy discussion of Corn Bill fixed duties and sliding scales:

Stop a bit. What did we decide? Is it to lower the price of bread, or isn't it? It doesn't matter which, but we must all say the same thing.

I know not how it is but mankind seem to have an aversion to the science of government. Is it because the subject is too dry? To me, no romance is more entertaining.

– John Adams

Occasionally from the hills above my home in Wales, when the weather is very brilliant, I can see the coast of Ireland, and sometimes then I fancy I discern the smoke of war upon that sad and lovely shore.

– Jan Morris

How I labored — how I toiled — how I wrote! Ye Gods, did I not write? I knew not the word 'ease'... Through good report and through ill report, I — wrote. Through sunshine and through moonshine I — wrote!

– Edgar Alan Poe,
The Literary Life of Thingum Bob. Esq.

PART FIVE

Countrymen

These "Countrymen" passages entered my Commonplace Book about a half-century ago. Re-reading them now, I find the passages brimming with wisdom, as I had when a student at law school.

Benjamin Franklin

Among his many professions, Franklin was a newspaper editor and printer. (And the possessor of a fine sense of humor.)

> – P.S. Gentle readers, we design never to let a Paper pass without a Latin Motto if we can possibly pick one up, which carries a Charm in it to the Vulgar, and the learned admire the pleasure of a Construing. We should have obliged the World with a Greek or two, but the Printer has no Types, and therefore we entreat the candid Reader not to impute the defect to our Ignorance, for our Doctor can say all the Greek Letters by heart.
>
> – New England Courant (1723)

> – Too many political leaders have the "mistaken opinion that the honour and dignity of government is better supported by persisting in a wrong measure once entered into than by rectifying an error as soon as it is discovered."

On the exchange of war prisoners:

- Edmund Burke, British statesman: If I were not fully persuaded of your liberal and manly way of thinking, I should not presume, in the hostile situation in which I stand, to make an application to you. But in this piece of experimental philosophy I run no risk of offending you. I apply, not to the ambassador of America, but to Dr. Franklin, the philosopher; my friend; and the lover of his species.

- Franklin: Since the foolish part of mankind will make wars from time to time with each other, not having sense enough otherwise to settle their differences, it certainly becomes the wiser part, who cannot prevent those wars, to alleviate as much as possible the calamities attending them.

In 1781, Franklin, John Adams and John Jay were chosen as Commissioners to negotiate peace with Great Britain.

Franklin to Adams: I have never known a peace made, even the most advantageous, that was not censured as inadequate, and the makers condemned as injudicious and corrupt. 'Blessed are the peacemakers' is, I suppose, to be understood in the other world; for in this they are frequently cursed.

– We must not expect that a new government may be formed as a game of chess may be played by a skillful hand, without a fault. The players of our game are so many, their ideas so different, their prejudices so strong and various, and their particular interests... seeming so opposite, that not a move can be made that is not contested; ... the wisest must agree to some unreasonable things that reasonable ones of more consequence may be obtained.

– I wish it were possible to invent a method of embalming drowned persons, in such a manner that they may be recalled to life at any period, however distant; for having a very ardent desire to see and observe the state of America a hundred years hence, I should prefer to any ordinary death, the being immersed in a cask of Madeira wine, with a few friends, till that time.

Franklin was the youngest of the ten Franklin brothers, and his sister, Jane Mecom, the youngest of the seven sisters. They outlived the others by twenty-four years and came to love one another "proportionably more" as they stood more and more alone.

– Franklin to Jane Mecom: I have long been accustomed to receive more blame as well as more praise, than I deserved. It is the lot of every public man, and I leave one account to balance the other.

– Jane Mecom to Franklin: I tell you these things that you may see I do In joy Life hear, … but oh may I not Live to hear of the Departure of My Dear Brother.

– Franklin to Jane Mecom: As to the Pain I suffer, about which you make yourself so unhappy, it is, when compared with the long Life I have enjoyed of Health & Ease, but a Trifle.

And it is right that we should meet with Something to wean us from this World and make us willing, when called, to leave it.

Otherwise the parting would indeed be grievous I am ever
Your affect Brother B. F.

– Franklin: I am going from the old world to the new; and I fancy I feel like those who are leaving this world for the next: grief at the parting; fear of the passage; hope of the future.

George Washington

Washington at age sixteen on a surveying trip to the Blue Ridge Mountains:

– This Morning went out and Survey'd five Hundred Acres of Land …. [On] our way Shot two Wild Turkies….

Last Night was a blowing and Rainy night Our
Straw catch'd a Fire yt. we were laying upon
and was luckily Preserv'd by one of our Mens
awakening when it was in a [blaze]....

Sits for his portrait in 1772:

– Inclination having yielded to Importunity, I
am now contrary to all expectations under the
hands of Mr. [Charles Willson] Peale; but in
so grave — so sullen a mood — and now and
then under the influence of Morpheus, when
some critical strokes are making, that I fancy
the skill of this gentlemen's Pencil, will be put
to it, in describing to the World what manner
of man I am.

To Congress, following his appointment as Commander
of the Army:

When we assumed the soldier, we did not lay
aside the citizen.

To the President of the Continental Congress:

– But why should I expect to be exempt from
censure...? Merits and talents, which I can
have no pretentions of rivalship, have ever been
subject to it. My heart tells me it has been my
unremitted aim to do the best circumstances

will permit; yet I may have been often mistaken in my judgment of the means, and may, in many instances deserve the imputation of error.

In 1792 Madison was requested to prepare a farewell address which Washington planned at that time to deliver upon the completion of his first term as President. Washington wished to have stressed that:

– "We are all the children of the same country — a country great and rich in itself — capable and promising to be as prosperous and as happy as any the annals of history have ever brought to our view.... Our interest, however diversified in local and smaller matters, is the same in all the great and essential concerns of the Nation....

(Washington later decided to serve a second term.)

Washington to Jefferson:

– Without more charity for the opinions and acts of one another in governmental matters..., I believe it will be difficult, if not impracticable, to manage the reins of government or to keep the parts of it together.

Washington to Hamilton:

– Differences in political opinions are as unavoidable, as, to a certain point, they may

perhaps be necessary. But it is exceedingly to
be regretted, that subjects cannot be discussed
without temper on the one hand, or decisions
submitted to without having the motives
… improperly implicated on the other; and
this regret borders on chagrin, when we find
that men of abilities, zealous patriots, … will
not exercise more charity in deciding on the
opinions and actions of one another.

– It is not the part of a good citizen to despair of
the republic.

To the President of the Continental Congress:

– Men are very apt to run into extremes. Hatred
to England may carry some into an excess of
confidence in France, especially when motives
of gratitude are thrown into the scale. Men of
this description would be unwilling to suppose
France capable of acting so ungenerous a part.
But it is a maxim founded on the universal
experience of mankind that no nation is to be
trusted further than it is bound by its interest;
and no prudent statesman or politician will
venture to depart from it.

To unpaid officers on the verge of mutiny:

– With respect to the advice given by the author
[of the Newburgh Addresses] to suspect the

man who shall recommend moderate measures
and longer forbearance, I spurn it.... If men are
to be precluded from offering their sentiments
on a matter which may involve the most
serious and alarming consequences that can
incite the consideration of mankind, reason is
of no use to us. The freedom of speech may be
taken away, and dumb and silent we may be
led, like sheep, to the slaughter.

From Farewell Address (1796):

> – Citizens, by birth or choice, of a common
> country, that country has a right to concentrate
> your affections. The name of american, which
> belongs to you, in your national capacity,
> must always exalt the just pride of Patriotism,
> more than any appellation derived from
> local discriminations. With slight shades
> of difference, you have the same religion,
> manners, habits, and political principles. You
> have in a common cause fought and triumphed
> together: the Independence and Liberty you
> possess are the work of joint counsels, and
> joint efforts of common dangers, sufferings,
> and successes.

Diary — last days, December, 1799:

> – 12th. Morning cloudy; wind at northeast;
> mercury 33. A large circle round the moon

last night. About one o'clock it began to snow; soon after, to hail, and then turned to a settled cold rain. Mercury 28 at night.

   – 13th. Morning snowing, and about three inches deep. Wind at northwest, and mercury at 30. Continued snowing till one o'clock, and about four it became perfectly clear. Wind the same place, but not hard. Mercury 28 at night.

On the evening of December 12th, George Washington caught the sore throat from which he died at 11 pm, December 14, in the sixty-eighth year of his life.

Thomas Jefferson

On drafting the Declaration of Independence:

   – Jefferson sought "not to find new principles, or new arguments, never before thought of, not merely to say things which had never been said before; but to place before mankind the common sense of the subject, in terms so plain and firm as to command their assent, and to justify ourselves in the independent stand we are compelled to take. Neither aiming at originality of principle or sentiment, nor yet copied from any particular and previous writing, it was intended to be an expression of the American mind, and to give to that expression the proper tone and spirit called for by the occasion."

From Jefferson's first Inaugural Address:

– During the contest of opinion through which we have passed, the animation of discussion and of exertions has sometimes worn an aspect which might impose on strangers unused to think freely and to speak and to write what they think; but this being now decided by the voice of the nation, announced according to the rules of the constitution, all will, of course, arrange themselves under the will of the law, and unite in common efforts for the common good. All, too, will bear in mind this sacred principle, that though the will of the majority is in all cases to prevail, that will, to be rightful, must be reasonable; that the minority possess their equal rights which equal law must protect, and to violate would be oppression. Let us, then, fellow-citizens, unite with one heart and one mind. Let us restore to social intercourse that harmony and affection without which liberty and even life itself are but dreary things. And let us reflect that, having banished from our land that religious intolerance under which mankind so long bled and suffered, we have

yet gained little if we countenance a political
intolerance as despotic, as wicked, and capable
of as bitter and bloody persecutions. During the
throes and convulsions of the ancient world,
during the agonizing spasms of infuriated
man, seeking through blood and slaughter his
long-lost liberty, it was not wonderful that the
agitation of the billows should reach even this
distant and peaceful shore; that this should
be more felt and feared by some and less by
others; that this should divide opinions as to
measures of safety. But every difference of
opinion is not a difference of principle. We
have called by different names brethren of the
same principle. We are all republicans — we
are federalists....

I'm all for Jefferson, he has the popular touch.
Of course he's read too many books, but I've
always said an idea or two won't sink our
Republic.   – Robert Lowell, Benito Cereno

Jefferson was 68 and Adams 76 when the two former
presidents began to correspond. For eleven years,
since the campaign of 1800, they had not been on
speaking terms. For the remaining years of their lives,
one hundred and fifty envelopes marked "President
Adams" and "President Jefferson" passed to and from
Monticello and Quincy.

Jefferson in reply to the first letter of Adams:

– A letter from you calls up recollections very dear to my mind. It carries me back to the times when, beset with difficulties and dangers, we were fellow laborers in the same cause, struggling for what is most valuable to man, his right of self-government. Laboring always at the same oar, with some wave ever ahead, threatening to overwhelm us,… we knew not how we rode through the storm with heart and hand, and made a happy port. Still we did not expect to be without rubs and difficulties; and we have had them….

But whither is senile garrulity leading me? Into politics, of which I have taken final leave. I think little of them and say less. I have given up newspapers in exchange for Tacitus and Thucydides, for Newton and Euclid, and I find myself much the happier. Sometimes, indeed, I look back to former occurrences, in remembrance of our old friends and fellow laborers, who have fallen before us. Of the signers of the Declaration of Independence, I see now living not more than half a dozen on your side of the Potomac, and on this side, myself alone. You and I have been wonderfully spared, and myself with remarkable health, and a considerable activity of body and mind. I am on horseback three or four hours of every

day; visit three or four times a year a possession
I have ninety miles distant, performing the
winter journey on horseback. I walk little
however, a single mile being too much for me;
and I live in the midst of my grandchildren,
one of whom has lately promoted me to be a
great-grandfather. I have heard with pleasure
that you also retain good health, and a greater
power of exercise in walking than I do. But I
would rather have heard this from yourself,
and that, writing a letter like mine, full of
egotisms, and of details of your health, your
habits, occupations and enjoyments, I should
have the pleasure of knowing that in the race
of life, you do not keep, in its physical decline,
the same distance ahead of me which you have
done in political honors and achievements. No
circumstances have lessened the interest I feel
in these particulars respecting yourself; none
have suspended for one moment my sincere
esteem for you; and I now salute you with
unchanged affections and respect.

Adams to Jefferson:

– I cannot be serious! I am about to write you
the most frivolous letter you ever read. Would
you go back to your cradle, and live over again
your seventy years?

Jefferson responds:

> You ask if I would agree to live my seventy
> or rather my seventy-three years over again?
> To which I say, yea. I think with you, that it
> is a good world on the whole; that it has been
> framed on a principle of benevolence, and
> more pleasure than pain dealt out to us. There
> are indeed, (who might say nay) gloomy and
> hypochondriac minds, inhabitants of diseased
> bodies, disgusted with the present, and
> despairing of the future; always counting that
> the worst will happen, because it may happen.
> To those I say, how much pain have cost us
> the evils which have never happened! My
> temperament is sanguine. I steer my bark with
> Hope in the head, leaving Fear astern.

When Jefferson succeeded Franklin as American
Minister to France, the French foreign minister
asked, "It is you who replace Dr. Franklin?" Jefferson
responded, "No one can replace him, Sir; I am only
his successor."

Jefferson and Adams died within hours of each other
on July 4, 1826 — the fiftieth anniversary of the
Declaration of Independence: Jefferson at age 83,
Adams at 90.

Abraham Lincoln

Autobiography:

– My father, at the death of his father, was but six years of age, and he grew up literally without education. He removed from Kentucky to what is now Spencer County, Indiana, in my eighth year. We reached our new home about the time the State came into the Union. It was a wild region, with many bears and other wild animals still in the woods. There I grew up. There were some schools, so called, but no qualification was ever required of a teacher beyond "readin', writin', and cipherin'" to the rule of three. If a straggler supposed to understand Latin happened to sojourn in the neighborhood, he was looked upon as a wizard. There was absolutely nothing to excite ambition for education. Of course, when I came of age I did not know much. Still, somehow, I could read, write, and cipher to the rule of three, but that was all. I have not been to school since. The little advance I now have upon this store of education, I have picked up from time to time under the pressure of necessity.

I was raised to farm work, which I continued till I was twenty-two. At twenty-two I came to Illinois, Macon County. Then I got to New Salem, at that time in Sangamon, now

in Menard County, where I remained a year
as a sort of clerk in a store. Then came the
Black Hawk War; and I was elected a captain
of volunteers, a success which gave me more
pleasure than any I have had since....

Lincoln speaking in Congress on the Black Hawk
war. (General Cass was the Democratic candidate for
President in 1848.)

– By the way, Mr. Speaker, did you know I am a
military hero? Yes, sir; in the days of the Black
Hawk war, I fought, bled, and came away.
Speaking of General Cass's career reminds me
of my own. I was not at Stillman's defeat, but
I was about as near it, as Cass was to Hull's
surrender; and, like him, I saw the place very
soon afterwards. It is quite certain I did not
break my sword, for I had none to break; but
I bent a musket pretty badly on one occasion.
If Cass broke his sword, the idea is, he broke it
in desperation; I bent the musket by accident.
If General Cass went in advance of me in
picking huckleberries, I guess I surpassed him
in charges upon the wild onions. If he saw any
live, fighting Indians, it was more than I did;
but I had a good many bloody struggles with
the mosquitoes, and although I never fainted
from the loss of blood, I can truly say I was
often very hungry....

– At what point shall we expect the approach
of danger [to our republican institutions]? By
what means shall we fortify against it? Shall
we expect some transatlantic military giant to
step the ocean and crush us at a blow? Never!
All the armies of Europe, Asia, and Africa
combined, with all the treasure of the earth (our
own excepted) in their military chest, with a
Bonaparte for a commander, could not by force
take a drink from the Ohio or make a track on
the Blue Ridge in a trial of a thousand years.

At what point then is the approach of danger
to be expected? I answer, if it ever reach us
it must spring up amongst us; it cannot come
from abroad. If destruction be our lot we must
ourselves be its author and finisher. As a nation
of freemen we must live through all time or
die by suicide....

– I am not an accomplished lawyer. I find quite
as much material for a lecture in those points
wherein I have failed, as in those wherein I
have been moderately successful. The leading
rule for the lawyer, as for the man of every
other calling, is diligence, leaving nothing for
tomorrow which can be done today. Never let
your correspondence fall behind. Whatever
piece of business you have in hand, before

stopping, do all the labor pertaining to it which can then be done.... Discourage litigation. Persuade your neighbors to compromise whenever you can. Point out to them how the nominal winner is often a real loser — in fees, expenses, and waste of time. As a peacemaker the lawyer has a superior opportunity of being a good man. There will be business enough....

– They [the Founding Fathers] meant to set up a standard maxim for free society, which should be familiar to all, and revered by all; constantly looked to, constantly labored for, and even though never perfectly attained, constantly approximated, and thereby constantly spreading and deepening its influence and augmenting the happiness and value of life to all people of all colors everywhere.

Letter from Lincoln to the Jefferson Dinner Committee of Boston:

– All honor to Jefferson — to the man who, in the concrete pressure of a struggle for national independence by a single people, had the coolness, forecast, and capacity to introduce into a merely revolutionary document an abstract truth, applicable to all men and all times.

– The true rule in determining to embrace or reject anything, is not whether it have any evil in it, but whether it have more of evil than of good.

– It is a struggle for maintaining in the world that form and substance of government whose leading object is to elevate the condition of men — to lift artificial weights from all shoulders; to clear the paths of laudable pursuit for all; to afford all an unfettered start and a fair chance in the race of life.

– It [the pardon] must be referred to the Attorney General, but I guess it will be all right, for me and the Attorney General's very chicken hearted.

– I shall never be old enough to speak without embarrassment when I have nothing to talk about.

– Tell Tad the goats and father are very well, especially the goats. (Telegram to Mrs. Lincoln)

– The part assigned to me is to raise the flag, which, if there be no fault in the machinery, I will do, and when it is up, it will be up to the people to keep it up.

Lincoln's response to the proposal that Confederate prisoners he treated as poorly as the Union prisoners in Andersonville:

Whatever others may say or do, I never can, and I never will, be accessory to such treatment of human beings.

* * *

– Let us discard all this quibbling about this man and the other man — this race and that race and the other race being inferior... and unite as one people throughout this land.

– How hard, oh, how hard it is to die and leave one's country no better than if one had never lived for it.

Artemus Ward was the pen name of C. F. Browne, a young writer and printer. Lincoln found relief and relaxation in the humor of Artemus Ward. On occasion he would open a Cabinet meeting by reading a selection.

Artemus Ward calls on President Lincoln:

– I called on Abe. He received me kindly. I handed him my umbreller, and told him I'd have a check for it if he pleased. "That," sed he, "puts me in mind of a little story. There was a man out in our parts who was so mean that he took his wife's coffin out the back winder for fear he would rub the paint off the doorway. Wall, about this time there was a man in a adjacent town who had a green cotton umbreller."

"Did it fit him well? Was it custom made? Was he measured for it?"

"Measured for what?" said Abe.

"Wall, as I was sayin," continued the President, treatin the interruption with apparent contempt, "this man sed he'd known that there umbreller ever since it was a parasol. Ha, ha, ha!"

"Yes," sed I, larfin in a respectful manner, "But what has this man with the umbreller to do with the man who took his wife's coffin out the back winder?"

"To be sure," said Abe — "what was it? I must have got two stories mixed together, which puts me in mind of another lit—"

"Never mind, Your Excellency. I called to congratulate you on your career which has been a honest and a good one — unscared and unmoved by Secesh in front of you and Abbolish at the back of you — each one of which is a little wuss than the other if possible!

* * *

I took my departer. "Good bye, old sweetness!" sed Abe, shakin me cordgully by the hand.

"Adoo, my Prahayrie flower!" I replied, and made my exit.

POSTSCRIPT

I visit my Central Park tree, a red oak planted in the 1920s on the East Green, just inside the park from 70th Street and Fifth Avenue. It is "mine" because the tree has been endowed in my name by board members of Volunteers of Legal Service on the occasion of my retirement in 2011, having served as executive director for 25 years.

For decades, I have spent weekend hours on the East Green, seated on the grass, leaning against the rough bark of this tree, writing and reading. From here I see the Frick Collection, the facades of Fifth Avenue apartment buildings, and a lovely park landscape.

My red oak is a proud, handsome tree, standing 60 feet tall. Its broad canopy has long provided me with beneficial shade. On hot summer days, I will continue to enjoy its shade and listen to the sound of its swaying branches. On summer nights, I will watch fireflies dart around the trunk. In the fall, I will admire its bright orange leaves and collect the acorns it sheds, placing them on a plate in my living room. In winter, I will visit my tree as it braves the elements.

The Portuguese writer, José Saramago, in <u>Small Memories, A Memoir</u>, describes his father late in life going "from tree to tree in his garden, embracing their trunks and saying goodbye to them, to their friendly shade...."

Late in my life, as the end draws near, I will embrace the trunk of my tree and say goodbye.

WRITERS ENRICHING
MY LIFE

John Adams

Aeschlyus

Anna Akhmatova

Caroline Alexander

Jean Anouilh

W. H. Auden

Honore Balzac

Julian Barnes

Samuel Beckett

William Blake

Jorge Luis Borges

James Boswell

James Boswell, Jr.

Adolph Brandeis

Bertolt Brecht

Benjamin Britten,
 E. M. Forster and
 Eric Crozier

Joseph Brodsky

Martin Buber

Luis Buñuel

Edmund Burke

Albert Camus

Anton Chekhov

Winston Churchill

William Johnson Cory

Robertson Davies

Dorothy Day

Agnes de Mille

Madame de Stael

Charles Dickens

Fyodor Dostoevsky

Elizabeth, the Queen Mother

Odysseus Elytis

Ralph Waldo Emerson

Jean-Henri Fabre

William Faulkner

Gustave Flaubert

Wallace Fowlie

Pope Francis

Benjamin Franklin

Carlos Fuentes

Mahatma Gandhi

André Gide

Jean Giraudoux

Goethe

Nikolai Gogol

Carlo Goldoni

Edmond and Jules
  de Goncourt

Maxim Gorky

Goya

Martha Graham

Julian Green

Comte Greffulhe

Hafez

Seamus Heaney

King Henry IV of France

Aleksandr Herzen

Homer

Horace

Langston Hughes

Leigh Hunt

Henrik Ibsen

Leoš Janáček

Thomas Jefferson

Michel Jobert

Pope John Paul II

Samuel Johnson

James Joyce

Ismail Kadare

Ryszard Kapuscinsk

Nikos Kazantzakis

John Keats

John Keay

Donald Keene

George Kennan

H. D. F. Kitto

Iraqi Kurds

Giuseppe di Lampedusa

Giacomo Leopardi

Mikhail Lermontov

Primo Levi

Abraham Lincoln

Robert Lowell

James Madison

William Maxwell

Jane Mecom

Lord Melbourne

Herman Melville

Michaelangelo

Czeslaw Milosz

Joan Miró

Gabriela Mistral

Moliere

Montaigne

Jan Morris

Vladimir Nabokov

R. K. Narayan

Pablo Neruda

Florence Nightingale

Michael Ondaatje

Eugene O'Neill

George Orwell

Charles Osborne

Orhan Pamuk

Boris Pasternak

Luigi Pirandello

Edgar Alan Poe

Aleksandr Pushkin

Sarvepalli Radhakrishnan

Rainer Maria Rilke

Graham Robb

Samuel Rogers

Franklin Roosevelt

Jalaluddin Rumi

Saint John

Saint Mark the Evangelist

José Saramago

Gaetano Salvemini

Leonardo Sciascia

Shakespeare

Ignazio Silone

Andrei Sinyavsky

Stephen Sondheim

Leo Stein

Stendhal

John Millington Synge

Henry David Thoreau

Thucydides

Titian

Leo Tolstoy

Ivan Turgenev

Vincent Van Gogh

Giuseppe Verdi

Virgil

Andrei Voznesensky

Artemus Ward
   (C. F. Browne)

George Washington

Walt Whitman

Richard Wilbur

Oscar Wilde

Thornton Wilder

Tennessee Williams

ABOUT THE
AUTHOR

William J. Dean is a lawyer, writer and civic participant. He lives and works in New York City.

As a lawyer, he has been deeply involved in the life of the city, having served for 25 years as the executive director of Volunteers of Legal Service, an organization providing pro bono civil legal services to benefit poor people in New York City.

As a volunteer, he has served as chairman, and now board member, of The New York Society Library, the oldest library in the city, founded in 1754; as former chairman and board member of the Correctional Association of New York, a civic association with statutory authority to visit and report on conditions in New York State prisons; and as the Wednesday night driver for the Coalition for the Homeless downtown food van for thirteen years. For two decades he conducted a forum series at the New School's Center for New York City Affairs, "New York: Problem City in Search of Solutions."

He is the recipient of the Brooke Russell Astor Award presented by The New York Public Library, an award honoring a person "who is relentless in his or her dedication to the City and who has contributed substantially to its enrichment."

Hundreds of his essays on a wide range of subjects have been published in leading newspapers. In 2013, a collection of 83 of his New York City essays were published under the title, My New York, A Life in the City. In 2014, his travel essays were published under the title, Into Distant Countries, Travels and Personal Journeys. He now serves as a monthly columnist for the magazine, Indian Economy & Market, published in Mumbai, India. The title of his column is "Letter From New York."

ACKNOWLEDGMENTS

Erin Tolman took on the enormous task of preparing a manuscript from hundreds of pages of my handwritten notes. She did this with energy, high intelligence and a strong literary background. Together we slogged through draft after draft. Thank you Jack Kraskopf for introducing me to Erin.

Elizabeth Sheehan then took the typed manuscript, with over 600 reading passages, and designed the book in an attractive and coherent way. Liz's diligence and enthusiasm are deeply appreciated. This is the third book we have worked on together.

With deep thanks to Krishna Kumar Mishra, Editor of the magazine, Indian Economy & Market, published in Mumbai, where my monthly column, "Letter from New York" appears, who encouraged me to proceed with this project.

To Joan Davidson who introduced me to the commonplace book of W.H. Auden, A Certain World, and encouraged me in this undertaking.

To Nelson Gutiérrez who took the photograph for the back cover and to Stephen Wilder for ongoing advice.

Also by the Same Author

My New York
A Life in the City

William J. Dean

A collection of personal essays on New York City. "These essays reflect my close ties to New York, the city forever a part of me."

Essay topics include:

> Walking, Central Park
> Grand Central Terminal
> Basketball and Opera
> Rikers Island and Potters's Field
> Bridges, Rivers, the Harbor
> Whitman and Thoreau in New York
> New York and Venice

Reader Comments :

"Anyone who has spent time in New York will find this a treasure trove of delightful surprises. It is beautifully written, with a rare combination of wit and deep feeling. It's a book every true New Yorker should have in his library."   — Thomas Fleming, Historian

"An absolutely lovely book. You can read any part of it and feel an instant sense of recognition for something you love about the city but were never able to articulate as clearly and elegantly as this."

                                        – Peter Cobb, Lawyer

This book is available from amazon.com

INTO DISTANT COUNTRIES
Travels and Personal
Journeys

William J. Dean

The title for my book comes from this passage of James Boswell in his Life of Johnson. "He [Johnson] talked with uncommon animation of traveling into distant countries; that the mind was enlarged it."

Part One of my book contains travel essays. I began with a trip around the world at age twenty and have not stopped since: Europe/Asia/Africa/Latin America, on business and pleasure trips. Travel has been a joy of my life. (I have been very spoiled. Johnson would have loved to visit Italy, but never got there, writing, "A man who has not been in Italy is always conscious of an inferiority.")

Part Two of my book contains travel essays of a metaphoric nature — not actual trips, but personal journeys as I call them — taken by me into other worlds: the worlds of literature, opera, social justice and teaching.

Reader Comment:
I found this book incredibly beautiful. Dean writes with the eye of a great artist, evoking lively memories of places I had been in my youth and leading the reader through the beauty of places I

had always wanted to see. Reading this book brings the reader the companionship of a friend who shares a fascinating knowledge of literature and history as he travels the world.

– Robert M. Pennoyer, Lawyer

This book is available from amazon.com

NOTES